Poverty, Household Food Security and Nutrition in Rural Areas

Poverty, Household Food Security and Nutrition in Rural Areas

Dr. (Mrs.) K. Uma Maheswari
&
Dr. (Mrs.) Vijaya Khader
Department of Foods & Nutrition,
College of Home Science
Andhra Pradesh Agricultural University
Rajendranagar, Hyderabad–500 030

DISCOVERY PUBLISHING HOUSE
NEW DELHI—110 002

First Published—2000

Reprinted-2011

ISBN 81–7141–519–9

Published by :

Discovery Publishing House
4831/24, Ansari Road, Prahlad Street
Darya Ganj, New Delhi—110 002 (INDIA)
Phone : 327 92 45
Fax.: 91-11-3253475

Laser Typeset by :

Allied Computers,
Karnal (Haryana)

Printed at:
Mehra Offset Press
Delhi

Preface

Impact of drought on crop production, productivity and income generation of farmers living in drought prone areas had been a subject of study of some importance. The information generated in the agronomic aspects of drought has been well documented from the study conducted at several State Agricultrual Universities and research institutions. Inspite of these studies, which have generated a fund of information, information of sociological aspects of drought, though attempted has been rather fragmentary and grossly inadequate. The occurrence of drought to which a few districts of Andhra Pradesh are repeatedly subjected to have varied impact on the marginal farmers and landless labourers. Many earlier studies have documented the large-scale migration of rural population and agricultural workmen and women to urban and semi-urban areas. The distress sale of possessions such as livestock and land also has been reported. But for those who have decided to stay back in the villages the drought period which extends to almost nine to ten months in an year is an extremely demanding one necessitating several measures to cope with the period of uncertainties and hardship. It is a welcome departure that the studies presented have attempted to analyse the different coping mechanisms adopted by the rural population to tide over the drought and its aftermath. Several interesting facts have come to light from the study. The information generated may also assist the planners, NGOs and the Government departments to evolve appropriate measures to ease the hardship of the people affected by drought which is of common occurrence in Ananthapur district, the area chosen for the study.

The authors deserves to be complimented for choosing a problem of great sociological relevance for their study, which affects the nutrition and health of rural population. Studies of this kind need to be enlarged to cover the other districts affected frequently by droughts and floods. It is hoped that such studies will be pursued with vigour in future years as they will be helpful in several ways for those who have the respsonsibility or commitment to bring succor to the affected population.

M. V. Shantharam

Acknowledgement

The authors expressed their sincere thanks to Dr. (Mrs.) P. Geervani, Vice Chancellor (Retd.), Sri Padmavathi Mahila Viswa Vidyalayam, Tirupathi for her keen interest in channeling this course of the study. We express our gratitude to Dr. Geervani for her learned council, valuable guidance and constructive criticism during the investigation period of this work.

We are thankful to the members of the advisory committee Dr. M. Narshima Reddy, Associate Professor, Extension Education Institute, Dr. P. Yosada Devi, Asst. Professor, College of Home Science, Dr. G. Nageswar Rao, Professor & University Head, Department of Statistics and Mathematics, College of Agriculture and to Sri A. Satyanarayana, Research Officer, Computer Centre, Acharya N. G. Ranga Agricultural University, Hyderabad for their guidance and help in the preparation of the manuscript.

We are thankful to the Director, Dr. R. Radha Krishna, and the staff of Centre for Economics and Social Studies, Government of Andhra Pradesh, Hyderabad for their guidance and cooperation.

We have pleasure in thanking the staff of Government Hospital, Kalyandurg, the Vysya Bank officials of the villages and the local village leaders without whose cooperation this work could not have been completed.

We sincerely acknowledge the cooperation extended by the respondents of the study. They expressed their utter destitution with many possible explanations which reflected in this piece of work.

We record our sincere thanks for all those who help directly or indirectly in bringing this work in the present form.

Authors

Acknowledgement

Author

Contents

1

Introduction

Food security can simply be defined as absence of hunger and malnutrition. Food security is a global problem. Globally there is enough food for all. The world dietary energy supply comes approximately to 2700 calories per person per day - well above what is needed to meet every one's energy needs. Data from FAO's food balance sheets (FAO, 1992) indicated that during 1989-90 dietary energy supplies averaged only 2070 calories in approximately 50 per cent of the poorest countries. Since 1947 India is facing several problems in ensuring food security, though 70 per cent of country's income is derived from agricultural.

Despite significant improvements in the world's food supplies, 195 million persons were below the poverty line rural areas during 1987-89, as per 43rd round of NSSO (Chauhan, 1994).

World food day was established in 1979 to "lighten pubic awareness of the nature and dimensions of the world food problem and to develop further the sense of national and international solidarity in the struggle against hunger, malnutrition and poverty.

India experienced, in 1987, what was labelled as the century's worst drought in terms of intensity as well as geographic spread. As many as 156 districts such as Srikakulam, Vizianagaram, Visakhapatnam, West Godawari, Krishna, Prakasam, Nellore,

Kurnool, Cuddapah, Rangareddy, Mahboobnagar, Nalgonda, Khammam, Guntur, Chittoor, Ananthapur, Adilabad and Nizamabad were declared drought affected in Andhra Pradesh.

Water scarcity and crop failure are the main distressing features of drought, resulting in primary deficit of food, fodder and drinking water. The other socio-economic symptoms of the scarcity situation are the lack of employment for the landless, small and medium farmers, migration of families in search of livelihood, mass migration of cattle, increasing indebtedness and distress sale of lands and possessions. The after effects of droughts are even more serious, than visualised. The affected farmers in distress sell their bullocks and other animals and migrate to cities in search of employment. When the rains come they are not in a position to plough their fields and grow crops. Even the seeds are not available for sowing the crops. Thus, the impact of drought has multiplying effect on the people (Kanwar, 1989).

The primary effect of drought is on agriculture, hence it's worst victims, from the stand point of nutrition, are the rural landless labours, small and medium farmers. Even in normal items (i.e., when the rainfall is normal) their diets are deficient in important nutrients (energy, vitamins and minerals) and drought imposes additional stress on them (Venkateswarlu, 1992). Among these communities within the household it is the preschool children and women who suffer most from dietary deficits. These categories are usually referred to as vulnerable groups even under normal conditions.

Several welfare programmes such as Integrated Child Development Services (ICDS), Public Distribution System (PDS), Jowahar Rojgar Yojana (JRY) and Development of Women and Children in Rural Areas (DWCRA) etc. have been implemented in drought prone areas to sustain food production and to contribute to food security. No matter how far reaching or effective government's intervention in the food sector may be, the ultimate responsibilities and penalties in the food system fall on people and their families, as a nations food security situation is the summation of the prospects of individual households. It is the households ability to obtain food that is critical is ensuring household food for security.

Over the years of famine and drought, households have developed some mechanisms to cope with scarcity. Households take the decisions out of past experience in coping with food insecurity. There are a few mechanisms which are applicable to most households in a given area.

Therefore, an understanding of the coping mechanism adapted for food security at household level in drought prone areas is essential to find out solutions fur future.

Andhra Pradesh is the fifth largest state in the country with 31.4 per cent of its population living below poverty line. The state is grouped into three broad socio economic and administrative regions viz. Coastal Andhra, Rayalaseema and Telangana. The Rayalaseema region is a zone of low rainfall, records an average annual rainfall of 672 mm. Ananthapur comes under Rayalaseema region (Status Report of NARP, 1994).

Ananthapur district was formed in the year 1952. The normal rainfall of district is 520.4 mm, by which it secures the least rainfall when compared to Rayalaseema and other parts of Andhra Pradesh. The failure of the rains leads the district to frequent droughts resulting in failure of crops.

Therefore, in order to understand the coping mechanisms adapted at household level in drought prone areas, Ananthapur district, Andhra Pradesh have been selected for the study.

Two rounds of survey was conducted in the present study to understand difference in coping mechanism operating between 'peak' and 'lean' seasons at household level by the families in this drought prone area.

Due to lack of rains, crop failure occurs which results in increase in the prices of commodities ultimately the consumption of foods like vegetables, milk decreases. Prolonged consumption of diets, which are deficient in calories and vitamins result in a steady decrease in food and nutrient intake in the vulnerable group of population. Therefore, the food & nutrient intake and nutritional status of women and pre-school children was studied.

Emergence of household food security is a concern, with the emphasis that 60-80 per cent of the expenditure of the poor is for food. The expenditure pattern of the people is the best yardstick to measure their living standards. Therefore food & non-food expenditure pattern of families were studied.

The study was conducted to understand the coping mechanisms adapted by landless, small, medium and large farm families and the food security situation of the families in four mandals of Ananthapur district the drought prone area, during 1993-94 with the following objectives :

General Objective

To assess the coping mechanisms adapted for food security at household level in drought prone area of Ananthapur district, Andhra Pradesh.

Specific Objectives

1. To assess the coping mechanisms adapted at household level for food security during acute food shortage periods in drought prone (dry land) area.
2. To assess the food & non-food expenditure pattern of the selected families in peak and lean seasons.
3. To assess the food & nutrient intake of women of child bearing age and pre-school children of small, medium and large farm and landless labour families in peak and lean seasons.
4. To assess the nutritional status of women and pre-school children of the selected families in peak and lean seasons.

2

Review of Literature

In the present study the review of literature is presented under the following sections :

- Coping mechanisms adapted for food security at household level
- Food and nutrient intake and nutritional status of the population in drought prone areas with special reference to women and pre-school children.
- Contribution of welfare programmes for food security.

Coping Mechanism Adapted for Food Security at Household Level

Household food security is the ability of the household to achieve sustained access is food of adequate quantity and quality for all household members (Kumar, 1995). Over the years of famine and drought households have developed some mechanisms and made the decisions out of past experience in coping with food insecurity.

The studies conducted on coping mechanisms of households for food security in drought prone area were reviewed under the following sub-headings :

— Food production based coping mechanism

a) Agricultural based coping mechanisms

b) Livestock based coping mechanism

— Employment, economic and income generation based coping mechanisms including food and non-food expenditure pattern.

— Asset (farm/non farm) based coping mechanism

— Food procurement, storage, preparation, distribution and consumption based coping mechanism

— General Studies

Food Production Based Coping Mechanisms

a) Agriculture Based Coping Mechanism

Studies Conducted in India

Ramaswamy (1988) in a study on coping with floods and drought explained that careful shifting of the past whether data could help in preparing for the worst possible situations by effective long term water-management arrangements.

Sahay (1990) analysed the *chakriya vikas pranali*, a multiplier planted system which was being practised in the drought-prone barren lands of certain villages of district Palamau in south Bihar, which changed the face of these villages from being one of the most barren into that of prospering ones. The most important feature of the pranali was that every drop of water gets retained, detained and used in this multi-cropping system of cultivation.

The study of Agarwal (1992) conducted in north-west India revealed that the integrated management of soil and water resources was of considerable importance for improving and stabilizing crop production particularly when rainfall was subnormal during crop season. Soil and water management practices such as tillage & seeding, weed control, compaction of deep sands, deep ploughing, use of brackish ground water, moisture conservation, rain water harvesting & reuse and proper fertilizer use played an important role in stabilizing and increasing the agriculture production in dryland areas.

Biman Basu (1992) suggested that as droughts develop gradually over months, providing enough the time to the people and the authorities to make adequate preparations, take (a) water

harvesting, (b) sprinkler irrigation and (c) use of drought resistant varieties of crops (d) fodder plants and (e) Establishment of fodder bank could considerably reduce the hardship of the affected people in drought prone areas. Indiscriminate deforestation and grazing by cattle and unscientific land use practices could all lead to a fragile ecological condition that was aggravated by lack of rain and leads to drought situation. It is now well established that trees help conserve moisture and inadequate rainfall. So intensive afforestation could bring back the rain and prevent recurring droughts.

Research results from the Dryland Agriculture Research Project (All India Coordinated Research Projected for Dryland Agriculture) showed that through intercrop and double crop systems production of pulses and oilseeds could be increased without unduly affecting the yields of cereals and millets (Singh and Ranganathan Chatty, 1991).

Venkateswarlu (1992) suggested the drought management strategies, such as alternative cropping strategies, tapping forest grasses increasing the area of fodder under irrigation, storage of adequate buffer food grains to meet the peak demands in drought periods, income general schemes, self-employment schemes and special health care programmes specially for children, expectant and nursing mothers.

Studies Conducted Abroad

Anderson (1981) suggested that income from the production of non food commodities such as cotton, rubber, coffee and tea played an important role in generating purchasing power among the poor and thus, improved their accesses to food and other basic needs (Anderson, 1981).

Immink and Alarcon (1992) conducted a study on household food security and crop diversification among small hold families in Guatemala and reported that two interrelated approaches were required, first productivity of basic food crops should be raised, second, the risks involved in production and marketing of cash crops should be lowered. Higher levels of fertilizer application and greater labour intensity in maize production might be expected to increase yields. Maize yield increase contributed a little to household dietary energy availability or to household income and thus to total household food availability. Higher bean yields were more likely to increase household dietary energy intake from own produced foods. Beans were often grown for household consumption. Household dietary energy intake from the farmers own production was more responsive to bean area expansion than to expansion in maize area so that substitution of beans for maize should have a positive net effect. Labour input per hectare were lower for beans, which was an important consideration on small holder farms. Beans have only 7 per cent less calories (per 100g of edible portion) than maize, but they have 2.5 times more protein and higher levels of many key micronutrients such as iron, calcium, thiamine, riboflavin, niacin and ascorbic acid.

b) Livestock Based Coping Mechanisms

Studies Conducted in India

Arora (1982) reported that keeping in view the erratic precipitation rate in Bondelkhand region of Uttar Pradesh, like other arid areas in the country, livestock farming, especially sheep farming played an important role as there were risks involved in the crop farming. It provided employment to a sizeable proportion of population through the wool and skin-based industry.

Govindaiah (1986) suggested the farmers in dryland areas in India to take animal husbandry enterprises as a subsidiary occupation, to get more income, that too a stable one. The animal husbandry activities could also provide employment to families where labour was underutilised. They could take any of the activities such as dairy farming, sheep and goat farming, poultry farming, rabbit raising etc.

Economic/Employment/Income Generation Based Coping Mechanisms

Studies Conducted in India

The study of Maheswari (1970) on children and women in Tirupathi, showed that as the income increased the total percentage of money spent on food decreased. However, There was a positive correlation between the income and expenditure on foods such as vegetables, pulses, fruits and animals foods. The consumption of cereals decreased with increasing income. Among the high income groups, foods like milk, vegetables, meat etc., were consumed to a greater extent than in the low income groups.

Snehalatha (1988) conducted a study on income, expenditure and saving patterns of rural households of Ibrahimpatnam mandal of Rangareddy District (A.P.) and reported that per family and per capita expenditure level for both food & non-food items increased with an increased in farm acreage. The percentage expenditure on food decreased with an increase in farm size. The per cent expenditure was almost same in case of small farm and labour families on all items. Out of the four categories of families only large farm families did get surplus income and other two categories were having deficit income over the consumer expenditures. The extent of savings were very meagre among labour and small farm families compared to large farm families. The magnitude of debts increased with the increased farm acreage.

Bidinger *et al.* (1990) study in Dokur, a drought prone village in the semi-arid Telangana region revealed that food grain price stability and the widespread availability of consumption credit permitted villages to maintain their consumption pattern of normal years. There were few viable public works projects in and around Dokur. However, at the height of the drought the village wage floor was in force to prevent women's wages from dropping below Rs. 3 (woman workers would have been attracted to locally available, rural works projects for wages as low as Rs. 3-4 per day). Moreover, labours were going to nearby villages in response to daily wage differentials as small one rupee. The cost of most making an investment in public works was reflected in the increase in rural indebtedness derived from the high demand for consumption credit.

Radhakrishna *et al.* (1991) analysed the rural labour markets in irrigated and dry zones of Andhra Pradesh and revealed that the participation rates of males aged 15-29 and 60+ were higher in the irrigated zone and the participation rates of females excluding 60 and children were higher in dry zone. The incidence of unemployment was higher in the irrigated zone. The wage rates were also significantly higher. The low incidence of unemployment and low wage rate in the dry zone could be due to the fact that the poor offer labour at low wage for survival and since, labour was available at low wage rate, they were employed by well off households for low productive activities like fuel collection, cattle rearing and other menial works. The labour in the irrigated zone was better organised and would also afford higher levels of unemployment without facing hunger.

Studies Conducted Abroad

Holy (1980), conducted a study on the effect of drought on tribal economy in western part of the Republic of Sudan. Traditionally the important sphere of production has been collecting wild growing gum arabic. One of the major effects of the drought on the Berti village economy was that during the very dry years of 1970 virtually all gum trees died, thus leaving many households without their important source of cash income, resulting in purchase of millets, other than the consumer goods.

John Mclntire (1981) reported that the monetary assistance scheme could provide more food security than grain reserves at lower costs as foreign exchange assistance would allow recipients to purchase the qualities of grain they want.

Reitsma Henk and Dietz (1992) compared the livelihood options and living conditions of the households in five small areas in Morocco, Keny, Togo, Mexico and Spain, the semi arid lands and reported that the important non-agricultural activities carried were cheese production (Pbasolo), baskets, (Papalutla), small scale artisanal production, food processing for sale (Togo), processing skins (Kenya), pottery (Togo, Morocco) and producing and selling sorghum beer (Togo, Kenya).

Asset based coping mechanisms

Studies Conducted in India

Muranjan (1991) studied the impact of 1987-88 drought on the socio-economic conditions of the rural people in Maharashtra and revealed that there was a greater reduction in the use of male labour and contractual labour than in the use of female labour. Drastic decline in the income from the cultivation land was compensated by the farmers, through other sources of income viz., employment as labour, sale of milk, sale of livestock and sale of other movable assets. On the whole the non-cultivating class was not affected as severally as the cultivating class. The large and medium farmers were affected more than the small and the marginal ones. Large farmers suffered a heavy decline in their income. The farmers sold livestock as well as other movable assets like gold, utensils, fuel from tress, bullock carts, implements etc. The marginal and the medium farmers sold both livestock and other assets whereas the large farmers were not. They continued with their reduced income. The small farmers sold only livestock as they had practically no other movable assets.

Food procurement, storage, preparation, distribution and consumption based coping mechanisms

According to Payne (1993) at the household level, coping responses for food security were behavioural rather than biological. They included redistribution of food among household members, redistribution of work over time to avoid mismatches between food needs and food availability. Households often use adaptive strategies, which lead them to be poor and stunted. He further reported that in hard times, working adults may temporarily lose body weight. This loss is an adaption to stress in the short run by using previously stored energy and in the long run by reducing food energy requirements for maintaining subsequent smaller body weight. A similar principle applies to small children. Inadequate food and frequent infection in the first two years of life usually mean that survivors face irreversibly slower growth and smaller adult body size. Although reducing the capacity for some forms of hard physical work, this again reduces the proportion of total energy expenditure and therefore, intake needed for maintenance.

Studies Conducted in India

Patel (1989) conducted a survey in 12 tribal villages in two districts of Maharashtra, affected by drought. A total of 7171 persons comprising 1442 households were surveyed. The author reported that the food mainly comprised rice diet and was devoid of pulses, vegetables, oils and fats. In most areas was hardly any grain in the stores in the individual houses. The drop in consumption level of the protected foods highlights the extreme poor quality of diet. The oil extracted from Mahua plant seeds was used, as other edible oil was too expensive. Prevalence of severe malnutrition was 25.2 per cent as against 5 per cent that was found normally in India, in under six population. Whereas the surveys in other drought affected areas showed prevalence of severe malnutrition as 15 per cent.

Bina Agarwal's (1990) study on poor rural families in India and their coping strategies associated with calamities such as drought and famine revealed that the effective coping mechanisms were the intra-household sharing of the burden of the coping and the appropriate state and non-state interventions that would straighten the survival mechanism adapted by the families themselves. Gender and age both form the basis of intra-family inequality. The burden of the coping falls disproportionately on female members within poor households, traceable to women's already weak and further weakened nutritional status during calamity.

In the 'Food for Development', news letters of the World Food Programme in India (1993), it was reported that in the village of Bijakura, a women named Jaklibai died after eating a poisonous wild tuber called 'Gethi' This was due to the consumption of poisonous roots, without destroying the poison by boiling it for 3 to 4 days.

Neela *et al.* (1994) study on rural women in Krishna Rakshit Chak in Midnapore district of West Bengal, India, revealed that women were the principal actors in the terms of collection of raw food, fruits, leaves, snails and fishes for meeting for deficits in households. The women were found to try to hedge against food availability, and tend to switch sources depending on the season. It was found that availability of rice, potatoes and pulses provided the primary food security to the people, in the sense that these sources of food were grown by the people. The secondary food security available to the people were existing natural resources such as produce from forests (fruits, wild tubers, wild beans, wild animals etc.).

Studies Conducted Abroad

In Ethiopia, a nutritional survey was conducted in Northern agricultural area over a 4 year period immediately before 1973, the year of famine. There was moderate migration of people from the rural areas to the road side towns. The energy intake indicated an extremely low nutritional status and this was exacerbated by an deficiency of vitamin A, goitre and lowered body fat reserves of the population (Miller *et al.*, 1975).

IFPRI (1983) studies revealed that the level of adequacy of the household diets tends to be better than the child's diet in cash cropping systems. An analysis of Kenya and Philippines studies showed that a doubling of household income could result in only a 9 percent and 4 per cent increase in energy consumption of pre-schoolers respectively. This was in households where pre-schoolers were consuming only 60-80 per cent of their energy needs. The data implied that large increase in household income would be needed in order to fill the energy gap in children's diets. It was found that increase in household income did not decrease illness. Children from the highest-income households. Since illness affects child's nutritional status the cash cropping schemes did not have a dramatic effect on pre-schooler nutritional status. It was found that in Kenya, as the household income increased, the vitamin A intake decreased. The reason was that, many of the vitamin A rich foods were seen as low prestige foods.

Finau (1985) conducted a study on food consumption pattern during a drought in Tonga by interviewing primary school children (7-8 years). Of the 158 children interviewed, 11 children reported hunger in their households and 4 children reported one meal per day. Carbohydrate consumption was high, but protein and vegetable consumption was low.

IFPRI (1986) studies in six countries, Gambia, Guatemala, Kenya, Philippines, India and Rwanda revealed that participation in export or cash crop production did indeed result in significant increase in household income. However, the increase in caloric consumption was less than expected. There was a tendency, as household income increased, to purchase more variety in the diet rather than more calories. It was also evident that 'lump-sum' sources of income, such as large payments for a cash crop or remittances were less likely to be spent on improving household food security and the 'lumpier' income flows had negative impacts on the food security of the household.

FAO (1989) report revealed that in Northern Brazil, the fruiting season of Babussu palm corresponded to the off-peak agricultural period. The fruits and kernels made significant contributions to the diet during this lean period (May *et al.*, 1985). In Senegal, wild foods were most commonly used to meet a seasonal food shortage at the beginning of the wet season (Becker, 1983). A survey in west Africa found that rhizomes, roots, tubers, were the main sources of energy in times of famine. Various types of bark, pith, buds, sap, stamps, leaves, fruit, flowers and seeds were also eaten (Irvine, 1952). In India, Malasia and Thailand, about 150 wild plant species have been identified as sources of emergency food. The kernels and bark of a number of forest species were ground into fine flour to make traditional *chapaties* (normally made out of wheat or rice flour) (FAO, 1983).

Food consumption based coping mechanisms were further discussed in detail, in 2.2 of this chapter, under the heading "Food and Nutrient intake of population in dryland and drought prone areas, with special reference to women and preschool children".

General Studies

Studies Conducted in India

Jodha (1975), Mascarenhas (1983) and Binswanger *et al.* (1984) conducted studies on the drought induced instability of food intake and nutritional, levels in Andhra Pradesh and reported that the first step in adjustment to drought was decline in food intake. A substantial decline in the consumption of food, particularly protective foods such as milk, vegetables, fruit and meat was observed in drought affected area of India. Shortage encouraged such practices as agreement to working as attached labour, insistence on wages in kind and seasonal migration.

Martha Alter Chen (1991), explored the specific vulnerabilities and responses of various household group in Maatisar village located in Dholka taluka in Ahmedabad district of Gujarat in Western India and reported that in coping with seasonality, most households attempted to protect themselves from shot-term reserves in income and subsistence flows. For additional support, households turned to family, kin and caste neighbors or drew upon common property resources. When all failed, households were forced to mortgage or sell assets. Most households guarded against long-term resort reverses in asset-holding and production potential. In peak season, caste neighbors frequently made small loans or gifts to one another. In slack seasons, these reciprocal or charitable transactions were narrowed from caste neighbours to kinship network. The demand and competition for common property resources increased while the quantity and quality of these resources decreased. About 50 households in the village migrated each year from early November to mid-March in search of work and 15 households migrated during other slack periods, showing clearly a latent demand for season public works on a regular basis.

Kalla *et al.* (1992) conducted a caste study on the coping strategies of households for food security in high risk environment in Rajasthan and revealed that the agricultural coping mechanism adapted by farmers were shifts in land utilization, resorting to repeat sowings, curtailment in fresh acquisition and sale of farm & non-farm assets & consumer durables, postponement of major repairs and resource improvement. The livestock coping mechanisms adapted was selling and gifting of livestock. The income generating coping mechanisms adapted were working in Government sponsored welfare programmes. The consumption coping mechanisms were curtailment in own produced product-mix, substitution of superior consumer goods, postponement of acquisition of consumer durables, curtailment in expenditure on entertainment, intoxication and social expenditure.

Karanth (1993) conducted a case study in a village of Chitradurga district, Karnataka, a drought prone area and analysed three broad areas of farmers survival strategies namely, the "frugal strategies", the "hard options" and to those who have not found the drought to be a problem. Frugal strategies comprised of minimising the use of hired labour of consumption, longer hours of grazing, use of non-conventional fodder and food, working as labours for number of days than usual, deferring various social and religious obligations, etc. Hard options consisted of migration in search of work, fodder & food, sale of assets, borrowing money and/or food grain, working as wage labourers, entering bonded labour services, etc. One of long term risk management strategy adapted was permanent migration to a region where droughts were not as frequent as in this region. A second risk management strategy was to irritate one's land specially by the big farmers. A third risk management strategy in practice was animal husbandry, specially sheep and goat rearing activities. The other strategies, adapted were leather-ware making, carpentry, smithy, rope and mat making etc.

Studies Conducted Abroad

Richards (1983) reported than the Mogbuama (a village of Africa) farm households adapted a number of agronomic strategies for fending off hunger, of which intercropping and planting early rice were the most important self-help strategies on the farm. Off-farm self-help strategies adapted were hunting and food gathering activities. Wild yam was used as staple in place of rice. Honey and bees wax were other gathered commodities which generated a small cash income. Tapping palm wine, preparing zin, trapping rodents by participating in pest control works, fishing and catching monkey (as monkey meat was valued in many households), and hunting game were the other strategies adapted. Labouring, gambling and theft for cash were also observed. When all prospects for self-help have been exhausted the hungry households turned to others for assistance, which took three forms : informal assistance among kin, pledging and formal borrowing on interest. With regard to help from kin, it was observed that some times close relatives only agreed to provide assistance. Borrowing was the last resort when all other resources were exhausted. When the normal surplus was inadequate to feed, the labour force was drawn into mining, the foreign exchange generated by mining allowed government to important rice.

Neumann *et al.* (1989) studied the response of 247 households to the impact of drought in Kenyan districts, in sub-saharan African countries and reported that the immediate response to hunger and the primary coping mechanism of households during the drought was to purchase food and others being curtailment of purchasing and sacrificing of assets and lands to survive.

Joachim *et al.* (1992) suggested that, households adapt a variety of coping mechanism to offset the effects of production shortfalls and market uncertainties. The first stage involved element of risk minimisation such as savings, investments, accumulation of assets, and diversification of income sources. The second stage involved disaccumulation of previous investments and taking loans.

Webb *et al* (1992) study revealed that in Ethiopian households, income distribution affected consumption which decreased one meal or less per day among 63 per cent of the poorest households, compared with only 43 per cent of the we all their group.

Alderman *et al.* (1993) conducted a longitudinal study for a three year period during 1986-89 and analysed the fluctuations in income, consumption, savings, nutrition and health seeking behaviour of 800 households in five districts of rural Pakistan and reported that out of the five source's of rural income namely agriculture, livestock, nonfarm, rental and transfers; agricultural income accounted for the largest share of overall income inequality. On the other hand, income from livestock and non-farm sources helped to decrease income inequality. Fluctuations in income did not translate into fluctuations in calorie intake. They cope with seasonal stress and higher food prices through savings including storage of grains. Credit mostly from the informal sector helped to maintain a fairly constant expenditure level. The study indicated that as householdsd income increased, diets were diversified with higher-quality foods rather than with larger quantities of food.

Food & Nutrient Intake and Nutritional Status of the Population in Drought Prone Areas with special Reference to Women and Preschool Children

Food & Nutrient Intake of Rural Population in Andhra Pradesh

Studies Conducted in India

NNMB (1990-1992) conducted studies on the diet and nutritional status of representative segments of different population groups in different states of India. During the year 1991, a total of 7373 households were covered and examined for nutritional status. The average intake of food & nutrients in Andhra Pradesh (cu/day) was given in Table 1. In all the states of India, surveyed cereals and millets formed the bulk of dietaries and their average consumption ranged from 372 to 598 grams per consumption unit.

NNMB (1984) studies revealed that between the diets of urban and rural people the diets of rural groups were far below than those of urban group. The consumption of protective foods like pulses, green leafy vegetables, milk products, egg and flesh foods were lower in rural areas compared to urban areas. The cereal intake was less in urban area than in rural areas. The food intake, both in rural and urban areas was less than the ICMR recommendation dietary allowance.

Within the rural groups, the landless labour group tended to consume nutritionally inferior diet. Even the level of energy—the basic nutrient, in their diets fell short of RDA (2400 Kcal/CU/day), leave alone minerals and vitamins. The calorie intake of landless

Table 1 : Average Intake of Food and Nutrients in Andhra Pradesh (*CU/day)

Sl. No.	*Food Groups (g/cu/day)*	*Andhra Pradesh*	*RDI ICMR (1989)*	*Nutrients (CU/day)*	*Andhra Pradesh*	*RDI ICMR (1989)*
1.	Cereals and millets	523.2	460.0	Calories (K.cal)	2247.0	2350.0
2.	Pulses	29.3	40.0	Protein (g)	53.1	60.0
3.	GLVs	5.9	40.0	Fat (g)	22.4	–
4.	Other vegetables	32.7	60.0	Calcium (mg)	447.2	400.0
5.	Roots and Tubers	28.5	–	Iron (mg)	24.8	28.0
6.	Nuts and oil seeds	3.5	–	Vit. A–retinol (ug)	235.7	600.0
7.	Fruits	38.5	–	Thiamine (mg)	0.7	1.4
8.	Fish and other flesh foods	6.8	–	Riboflavin (mg)	0.7	1.4
9.	Milk	80.1	150.0	Vitamin C (mg)	30.9	40.0
10.	Fats and oils	10.8	40.0			
11.	Sugar and jaggery	10.6	30.0			

* The calorie consumption of an average adult men, weighing 60 kg., doing sedentary work is taken as one consumption unit.

agricultural labour group as revealed by the diet surveys conducted by NNMB (1988-1990) was only 2310 Kcal/Cu/day.

Food & Nutrient Intake and Nutritional Status of Women and Pre-School Children

Studies Conducted in India

The average nutrient intake of adult women in Andhra Pradesh is given in Table 2.

Table 2 : The Average Nutrient Intake of Adult Women in Andhra Pradesh

Nutrients	*NNMB Data 1978*	*NNMB Data 1979*
Proteins (g)	59.60	64.70
Calories (Kcals)	2527.00	2600.00
Iron (mg)	28.00	32.60
Vitamin A (ug)	313.00	415.00
Thiamine (mg)	1.03	1.05
Riboflavin (mg)	0.71	0.88
Vitamin C (mg)	20.00	41.00

Source : NNMB (1978–79)

A study was conducted by Devadas *et al.* (1980) on food intake of 700 children in the age group of 0–6 years in a rural area of Coimbatore. It was found that the food intake of children was inadequate and the general nutritional status was below the Indian standards.

Pushpamma *et al.* (1981) study in three regions of Andhra Pradesh revealed that the nutrient intake of preschool children was far below the recommended allowance of ICMR suggested values.

Thimmayamma *et al.* (1982) studied a total of 574 subjects from 176 families in urban areas and 783 subjects from 171 families in rural areas around Hyderabad and reported that the calorie adequacy in the rural preschool children was 83 per cent irrespective of income level.

Devadas *et al.* (1983) studied 400 children of 0-6 years of age in rural areas of Andhra Pradesh for their nutrient intake. The intake of all foods was less than the ICMR recommended allowance. The consumption of leafy vegetables, fats & oils, sugar & jaggery were less than the recommended dietary allowance. The mean weight, height and arm circumference of the children were below the standard measurements.

Bhat *et al.* (1985) investigated 200 preschool children of 1-5 years in Gangwa village, Hissar district and reported that the diet of the children was deficient in protective foods. About 77.5 per cent children showed symptoms of nutritional deficiencies. Vitamin A deficiency was found to be widely prevalent among all age groups (40%), about 15 per cent children were found to suffer from third degree malnutrition and showed signs of severe protein energy malnutrition. The hemoglobin levels was found to be lower than the normal in children.

NIN (1986) conducted a study on the growth status of 1-5 year old children belonging to different socio-economic groups in Calcutta. The percentage prevalence of severe degree malnutrition was found to be 6.6 per cent in rural children.

Kakkar *et al.* (1987) study on nutritional status of 100 preschool children (1-5 years old) in two villages of Hissar district, revealed that only 18 percent of children had normal weight and the values of hemoglobin was found to be below as compared with normal value reported by WHO.

Nagamalleswari (1989) study on the women and preschool children in the villages of Rangareddy district, a drought affected area of Andhra Pradesh revealed that the cereal intake was more than the recommended allowances. Consumption of pulses, green leafy vegetables, milk, fats, & oils and sugar were far below the recommended daily allowances. Fish, meat, egg and fresh fruits were absent in their diets. The diets were deficient in all nutrients except protein and B complex vitamins. Calorie intake was also not meeting the RDI because of low intake of fats and oils. Consumption of more cereals improved the protein intake (71-100 proteins requirement met). Intake of calcium, iron, vitamin A, and B-complex vitamins (thiamine and riboflavin) were much below the requirement because of low consumption of milk & milk products and green leafy vegetables. The anthropometric measurements of children were lower than the ICMR (1971) standards and Harvard standards. Heights of children were lower than the ICMR and NNMB reported values which showed the past malnutrition. Chest circumference also showed slight difference. Only 8.5 per cent of children surveyed were normal children (normal weights for age), 26.3 per cent were in the Ist degree malnutrition, 50.6 per cent in IInd stage malnutrition and 14.5 per cent of children were severely malnourished.

Study conducted by Braun *et al.* (1992) revealed that while income differences did result in a large difference in the prevalence of food energy deficiency in many remote rural areas, household income differences were not making much of a difference to the levels of malnutrition of children in short run. Calorie deficiency was addressed effectively with household income growth.

The percentage prevalence of nutritional deficiency cases in preschool children in Andhra Pradesh as reported by NNMB (1990-92) were Oedema (0.0), Emaciation (0.9), Marasmus (0.7), PEM (0.3), Bitot spots (0.5) and Angular stomatitis (6.2). Angular stomatitis was more prevalent in Andhra Pradesh compared to other nutritional deficiency symptoms. PEM and vitamin A deficiency were next in the order of prevalence.

Studies Conducted Abroad

The influence of seasonal variations in dietary intake and nutritional status of preschool children was examined in a longitudinal study of approximately 20 women-children pairs in rural Bangladesh. Maternal and child nutritional status exhibited seasonal variations. Maternal nutritional status also varied by land holding.

Swaminathan *et al.* (1973) assessed the nutritional status of about 1,700 refugees from Bangladesh in three camps in West Bengal. The predominant deficiency was protein calorie malnutrition and the problem was very severe in the children under five years. The per cent prevalence of severe malnutrition among the refugee children as judged by body weight deficit was nearly double (35.5%) that was observed in Indian children under normal conditions.

Krishnamachari *et al.* (1974) assessed the food and nutrition situation in some drought affected areas of Maharashtra state

During 1973. The results showed that nutritional problems encountered in the area were protein-calorie malnutrition among preschool children, oral lesions of vitamin B- complex deficiency, anaemia and occular manifestations of vitamin A deficiency. The dietary intake was predominantly of cereals with negligible amount of good quality foods., Due to non-availability of jowar (usual staple of the area) the consumption of wheat and maize (unusual cereal) was found to be high. No deaths due to starvation were reported in the area.

Ashturkur *et al.* (1977) studied the nutritional status of 40 farm families in Parbhani district of Maharashtra. The study revealed that the consumption of all foods was less than 50 per cent of recommended except cereals which more than the recommended quantities. The diet of children consisted of more pulses. Consumption of fruits, oil and fat was much less than the recommended allowances.

The diets of 18 families representative of the communities residing in a village of North Arcot were studied by Sundarraj and with landless women weighing an average of 39.9 kg compared to 41.9 kg for women in landholding families (Lincoln *et al.*, 1979).

Food & Nutrient Intake and Nutritional Status of Population in Drought Prone Areas

Studies Conducted in India

Swaminathan *et al.* (1967) assessed the effect of drought conditions on the dietary intake and nutritional status of the population in three drought prone districts of Andhra Pradesh i.e. in Anantapur, Chittoor and Kurnool in 1966 and reported the protein calorie malnutrition, clinical signs of vitamin B-complex deficiency, anaemia and vitamin A deficiency in preschool children. The prevalence of corneal xerosis among the preschool children was quite high. No deaths due to starvation were reported in the area.

Swaminathan *et al.* (1969) conducted a study on food and nutrient situation in the drought affected area of Bihar and reported of intakes of cereals; consumption of wild green leafy vegetables, and consumption of wheat and millet which were not normally consumed. About 20 per cent of the families had per capita daily intake of the calories less than 1000 Kcal. The major nutritional deficiencies observed were protein calorie malnutrition among preschool children, anaemia, ocular signs of vitamin A deficiency and oral lesions of vitamin B complex deficiency in all age groups. There were no reports of deaths due to starvation in the areas surveyed.

Periera (1977). They found that the adult intake was in adequate in calories, Vitamin A, riboflavin and marginally deficient in protein. The diets were inadequate in thiamine, niacin and vitamin C.

Anurag Chaturvedi (1983) conducted a study on utilization of groundnuts in dryland region of Andhra Pradesh and revealed that owing to replacement of part of the cereals and pulses by groundnuts in the groundnut cultivating areas, the intake of calories, protein and niacin was higher.

Ramnath *et al.* (1983) study in the Andhra Pradesh state revealed that 80 per cent of the total calories were derived from cereals and millets. The contribution of other foods to total calories was very small, about 5 per cent each by pulses and milk. With increasing income the cereals millet contribution to total calories decreased. The families where the income was less than Rs. 2/- per capita per day, the contribution of cereal + millet to total calories was 75 per cent, while that of families with Rs. 5/- per capita per day was around 48 per cent.

Rama Devi (1986) conducted a study on the food and nutrient intake of sorghum and non sorghum eating families in Andhra Pradesh and found that the per capita income and per capita expenditure on all non food items and food items cereals and pulses was more among non sorghum eating population compared to sorghum eating population. In both the groups the percentage expenditure on food increased with a decreased in income. Both the groups spent maximum amount on food, 69 per cent and 55 per cent in sorghum and non sorghum eating population, respectively. The intake of cereals and pulses was more, while the intake of protective foods such as vegetables, fruits and milk was less among sorghum eating population. The intake of nutrients such as calories, protein, carbohydrates, iron, thiamine and niacin was more among sorghum eating population compared to non sorghum eating population. The diet of sorghum eating population was adequate with most of the nutrients except calcium, carotene, riboflavin and ascorbic acid. The non sorghum eating population showed adequate intake of fat, calcium and niacin while the intake of other nutrients was slightly below the recommended allowances.

Sailaja (1986) conducted a comparative study on the nutritional status of sorghum and non-sorghum eating families in Andhra Pradesh and found that higher per cent of the non-sorghum eating subjects had garde, I, II and III malnutrition and higher per cent of sorghum eating subjects were found to be normal. Anthropometry in general indicated that sorghum acting subjects had proportional deficits of weight, arm, chest and head circumferences confirming that these subjects had past chronic malnutrition. Higher per cent of non-sorghum eating subjects had anaemia and Vitamin A deficiency as compared with sorghum eating group. Angular stomatitis was more among sorghum eating groups. The intake of pulse and niacin was found to be more in sorghum eating families.

NIN (1987) conducted a survey in the states of Gujarath, Orissa, Andhra Pradesh, Tamil Nadu and Karnataka and assessed the impact of drought on the nutritional status of the affected people. Many of the districts covered in different states were the areas where drought conditions of varying degrees prevailed. Both during drought and non drought conditions, most food items except staple cereal and millets were being consumed much below the recommended level. During the drought, consumption levels of almost all food items in all the states were lower compared to non drought levels (NNMB, 1981). In Gujarath, a slight rise in cereal consumption was noted during drought. The extent of reduction during drought in the levels of consumption in case of milk, pulse, sugar and jaggery was drastic in some of the areas surveyed for example, milk in Andhra Pradesh, Gujarat, Karnataka. Large scale consumption of wild leaves and tubers (famine foods) eaten in distress conditions was not noticed. The diets were deficient in energy and vitamin A in all the states. Protein intake which was normal during non-drought period (NNMB) was also deficient in 3 of the 5 states surveyed. The variations seen in the nutrient intake reflected the difference in the intake levels of millets i.e., bajra in Gujarat and ragi in Karnataka. Except in Gujarath, in all the other states mean weight during drought period was lower than the non-drought period. In case of preschool children (1-5 years) the prevalence of severe grade of malnutrition was about 3 times higher in Mahaboobnagar during the drought. Such drastic change was not observed in other states.

During the drought of 1987, the Desert Medicine Research Centre (ICMR) carried out studies in a selected sample of 11,856 population living in the six desert districts in the western Rajasthan and reported that the mean deficit in calories in the preschool children varied from 600-900 Kcals/day. Adults too and marginal calorie and protein deficit. An average about 9-10 per cent of preschool children had grade 3 undernurition. Clinical evidence of vitamin A deficiency was the most significant problem. Night blindness was evident in varying frequencies. Evidence of clinal deficiency signs of the nutrients such as B complex and iron was alos seen in adults and children (Krishnamachari, 1989).

Thomas Walker and James (1990) studied the village and household economics in India's Semi-arid tropics (SAT) and reported that the primary deficiencies in diets were vitamin C, vitamin A, calcium, riboflavin and energy across the six study villages. The proportions consuming less than 50% RDA for calories ranges from 11-15% for children (1-12 years), 2-9% for males more than 12 years and 3-8% for females > 12 years. Severe cases of malnutrition among preschool children ranged from 2-7% across seasons and villages. Calorie deficiencies were most pronounced among 1-3 year old children. About 8% of individual fell < 70% of their age-sex weight for - higher standards. Evidence for a gender bias within age, season, and farm-size groups was not significant. Seasonal difference in meeting 50 per cent RDA in the age by sex by nutrient group comparisons were also not pronounced. Intake of thiamine, ascorbic acid, sulfur-amino acids, protein and calories were subjected to the extent of the seasonal variability, while consumption of beta carotene and lysine fluctuated the least. The incidence of mild and severe malnutrition also did not display a marked seasonal pattern. Vegetable production, the main source of ascorbic acid intake, was both inadequate and subject to substantial seasonal variation in all the villages. A proportional change in household expenditure was accompanied by a similar proportion increase in the quantity of food consumed. The households with larger landholdings had higher energy and nutrient intake than individuals from landless and small farm households. Effect of seasonality on children's nutrient intake was not empirically persuasive. Calcium intake decreased. B-carotene intake increased.

The study of Bidinger *et al.* (1990) in Dokur village of semiarid Telangana region, revealed that although physical health did not deteriorate during the drought, malnutrition, as manifested by less than adequate energy consumption was still evident, particularly among the most vulnerable younger age groups. Malnutrition was reflected in a decrease in weight for height between the first and second drought years.

A study was conducted by All India Coordinated Research Project in Foods and Nutrition on "Food and Nutrition situation of rural families in Seven Agro-climatic zones of Andhra Pradesh (1992-93). It was found that in scarce rainfall zone of A.P. (500-700 mm) the millet were consumed by all families. Intake of green leafy vegetables, fruits and oil was very low and below the RDI. Though milk intake was low in landless families, their intake of flesh food was more. Nuts and oilseeds were used to some extent by all families. The energy intake was lower than the RDI. Intake of iron, riboflavin and β-carotene was far the RDI. Heights and weights of adult women were normal, but BMI was low in women belonging to landless families. Preschool children was found normal as per their height/age and weight/height. Twenty five per cent of girls in small farm families were found suffering from grade III malnutrition. Deficiency signs of anaemia were noticed in adult women.

Studies Conducted abroad

After prolonged drought in the Bas-zaire region of Zaire in 1978 the resulting malnutrition was almost exclusively of protein and energy. Cassava supply was insufficient to feed young children who receive only after the needs of men in the households were met (Kamany *et al.*, 1978.)

Biellik *et al.* (1981) studied the mortality, nutritional status and dietary conditions in the food deficit region, north Teso district, Uganda, a drought prone area in 415 randomly selected children < 110 cm in height. A prevalence of 0.2 per cent moderate acute malnutrition was found.

Contribution of Welfare Programmes for Food Security

Studies conducted in India

Rao *et al.* (1988) reported that the national public works programmes provided only one third of the employment needed to protect the income.

Pramila (1989) compared the expenditure pattern and food & nutrient intake, anthropometry and clinical signs of 100 each of DWCRA beneficiary families and non-DWCRA families in Srikakulam district (A.P.). Per capita income was more among Non-DWCRA families compared to DWCRA families. Per capita expenditure on all food items except cereals, pulse, fleshy foods were more among Non-DWCRA families compared to DWCRA families. The intake of cereals, pulse, green leafy vegetables, animal foods and milk was more among DWCRA families. The intake of calories, protein, calcium, thiamine was more among DWCRA families. Deficiency signs of vitamin A and riboflavin were observed in the both groups. Some positive results were observed with regard to the anthropometric measurements of the members of the DWCRA families, but they were not significant.

Jodha (1989) reported that during the year 1987 drought, the Rajasthan State Government engaged relief works to labour to create private assets (irrigation wells, houses etc.) Except for wages, other costs were borne by the private beneficiaries.

Muranjan (1991) studied the impact of 1987-88 drought on the economic conditions of Rural people in Maharashtra and revealed that the reduction in cereal production was compensation by the supplies through public distribution system.

Because of the implementation of several targeted poverty allevation programmes, during the decade from 1978, the average Indian per capita income was increased. Since the mid-1970s just as food production had been fairly stable at the household level, calorie and other nutrient composition has remained more or less unchanged. It was observed from the NNMB (1990) data that the calorie consumption per adult ws markedly increased, which may be attributed to the proper implementation of PDS as well as poverty allevation programmes, such as the National Rural Employment Programme (NREP) and the Integrated Rural Development Programme (IRDP) (Second Report on World Nutrition Situation, 1993).

An assessment study of the impact of droughts on rural economy in Haryana revealed that the drought relief programmes included supply of drinking water to water drficit villages, supplementary nutrition programmes for children and expectant mothers, subsidised sale of fodder and inputs, filling of dry ponds with canal water and employment generation schemes etc. (Rangaswamy, 1992).

Studies conducted Abroad

The Ethiopian Relief and Rehabilition Commission set up in 1974 had taken steps to alleviate the problem of malnutrition by distribution food, improving roads, building air strips through food for work schemes and supplied clothing and medical assistance. In some areas they developed long term strategies designed to relieve population pressure on the land (Miller *et al.*, 1984).

Koester (1986) investigated that regional cooperation improved food security in nine African countries that joined the Southern African Development Coordination Conference (SADCC), by integration their agricultural markets, and cooperating in risk reducing activities, because fluctuations in cereals production, cash crop production and export earnings were smaller on the regional than national level. Based on past fluctuations in cereal production and import prices, the amount of stocks needed for each county to stabilize cereal consumption was calculated and this was compared to the stocks required by the same countries cooperating regionally. Results showed that regional stocks could be about 41 per cent less than the sum of national stocks without cooperation.

Frengley *et al.* (1992) studied the financial stress and consumption expectations among farm households in Newzealand and revealed that the financial assistance by the government to the Newsealand Agriculture resulted in a market improvement in the economic conditions. It was also observed that withdrawn of support for agiruclture rapidly decreased the net income and equity of farmers, causing significant stress in the farming community. A principal cause of financials stress affecting farm families was the constraint imposed on household consumption by farm debt. Interest costs threaten the financial viability of the 60 per cent of sheep and beef farmers whose debts exceeded 20 per cent of the total farm assets.

Braun's (1993) study in Africa revealed that the labour intensive public works addressed three central problems i.e., food security, growing unemployment and poor infrastructure and ensure direct and sustainable poverty alleviation and strenghtening-

capacities for self reliance. Malnourished rural poor Africans depended on non-agricultural sources for 40 to 60 per cent of their income. The effect of public works programmes on growth and the immediate alleviation of poverty made these programme attractive.

3

Materials and Methods

Ananthapur district is one of the dryland districts of Andhra pradesh formed in 1952. The district lies between 13^0–40' and 15^0–15' Northern latitude and 76^0–50' and 78^0–30' Eastern longitude with a population density of 133 per sq. km. as against 192 sq. km. of the State. The total geographical area of the district is 47.28 lakhs acres (Hand book of Statistics, Ananthapur district, 1991-92 and 1992-93). The normal cultivated area of the district is 22.00 lakhs acres, out of which 19.07 lakhs acres is under kharif season and 2.93 lakhs acres under Rabi season during the year 1989-90. During the year 1989-90, the total area under the food crops forms about 12 per cent to the total cropped area of thc districts. The total area under non-food crops works out to 88 per cent of the total cropped area of the district. The soils in Ananthapur district are predominantly red soils. Groundnut is the major crop accounting for 56.8 per cent of the gross cropped area. Jowar, rice, bajra, redgram and horsegram are other important crops. The district receives the lowest rainfall in Andhra Pradesh State (520.4 mm), as against 817 mm for the state (Census Book, 1993-94). The district occupies the lowest position in Andhra Pradesh and the second lowest position in India in rainfall. The average rainfall from 1980 onwards for eleven years is as low as 495 mm and therefore is prone to successive droughts (District Plan : Ananthapur, 1993).

Selection of Mandals

Four interior mandals which are known to have low rainfall (500–750 mm) consistently over the last three years (1991–93) from Ananthapur district of Andhra Pradesh were selected. The mandals selected were Kundurpi, Kambadur, Bramhasamudram and Amarapuram.

Selection of Villages

List of the villages in the 4 selected mandals were obtained from mandal revenue office and two villages were selected at random from each mandal. The villages selected from each of the selected mandals were as follows:

	Mandal	Villages
1.	Kundurpi	a) Kundrupi b) Enumuladoddi
2.	Kambadur	a) Noothimadugu b) Kadiridevunipalli
3.	Bramhasamudram	a) Brahamasamudram b) Kannepalli
4.	Amarapuram	a) Hemavathi b) Maddenakunta

The village profiles with all the details were collected from the concerned mandal offices and the district offices by using a structured schedule.

Selection of Households

By using a structured and pre-tested schedule, a household survey was conducted to screen the families having atleast one woman of chilo bearing age and one preschool child (1–5 years) from all the selected villages.

From the identified families of all the villages, 324 families were selected randomly on the basis of size of land holding.

Out of the total 324 families initially selected for the study, only 300 families were covered in the final study. The reasons for non-coverage of all the selected families are :

a) Non-availability of families on repeated contacts

b) Non-cooperation of a few families even after detailed explanation of the purpose of the study

c) To ensure equal number of large, medium, small farm families, landless labour families and landless labour families of JRY beneficiaries.

The land owned particulars of the families selected are shown in Table 3. Based on land holding size households were categorised as small (<5.00 acres), medium (5.00-10.00 acres) and large farmers (510.00 acres) households. Land holdings were first converted into standard acres based on the conversion formula given by Andhra Pradesh Government Land Reforms Act (1973).

Table 3 : Frequency Distribution of Families According to Ownership of Land

Land holding particulars	*Number of families*	*Average land holding per family (in acres)*
< 5 acres (SF)	60	2.24
5 – 10 acres (MF)	60	5.32
> 10 acres (LF)	60	12.49
Average		6.68
No land	120	—

Collection of Data

A preliminary survey was carried out by conducting a participatory rural appraisal (PRA) technique in the study area and arrived at the various copies mechanism adapted by the families for food security at household level. These mechanisms were categorised into eight major groups and based on the these a suitable schedule was framed specifically for the study to elicit information on coping mechanism adapted for the food security by the households.

The schedule prepared pertaining to the coping mechanisms adapted was pretested in the field and necessary modifications were made accordingly. The information and data pertaining to the year 1993-94 was collected with the help of the schedules. Mother of the preschool child was interviewed by home visits. Before collecting data, rapport was built up with the respondents by repeated visits to the village and by explaining the purpose of the study. The study was conducted once during the peak season (September to January) and once in lean season (March to July) of the year.

Food & Nutrient Intake and Nutritional Status Assessment

The primary effect of drought is on agriculture, hence its worst victims from stand point of nutrition are the rural landless labourer, small and medium farmers. Even in normal times (i.e. when the rainfall is normal) their diets are deficient in important nutrients (proteins, fats, vitamins and minerals) and drought imposes additional stress on them. Among these communities, within the household it is the preschool children and women who suffer most from dietary deficits. These categories are usually referred as vulnerable groups even under normal conditions. Therefore, food & nutrient intake and nutritional status of women and preschool children were analysed in this study.

Diet survey and nutritional status assessment by nutritional anthropometry of women and preschool children was carried out on 30 per cent of the selected samples. As the sample size was small to show the variations, clinical assessment was conducted in all the 300 selected sample of women and preschool children. Diet survey and nutritional status assessment was conducted in two seasons i.e. "peak" and "lean" seasons.

Diet Survey

Information on food intake pattern of women and preschool children was collected by 24 hours recall method by using a set of standardized diet survey vessels. The total family intake was recorded and also the individual intake for the mother of the preschool child and the preschool child of the family was recorded. The nutrient intake of the individual per day was calculated from standard food composition tables (Gopalan *et al.*, 1993).

β carotene, a precursor to vitamin A was measured in this study, because it is mainly derived from vegetable sources which are the predominant precursors of vitamin A in Indian diets, rather than, from fleshy foods which contain preformed vitamin A. The vitamin A content of fleshy foods and dairy products was converted into units of B-carotene.

Nutritional Status Assessment

Nutritional status of the selected families was assessed using anthropometric techniques and clinical observations.

Anthropometry

Anthropometric measurements namely weight and height for women, weight, height and mid arm circumference for preschool children of the selected families were recorded.

Weight

The weight of the subject was recorded using a standard weighing mahine (weight bird spring balance) with 100 g division. It was recorded always one or two hours after meals with light clothing.

Height

The height of the subject was measured by using a standard vertical manuring rod with 0.1 cm division. At the time of recording, the subject was asked to stand erect with heels together on a flat floor.

Mid arm circumference

The mid arm circumference measurements were taken by using non stretchable tape marked in cms with 0.1 cms division. The upper mid arm circumference of the left hand was taken, placing the hand parallel to the body without movement.

Body Mass Index (BMI)

The Body Mass Index (weight in kg/height in meters^2) was used as an indicator of nutritional status of the women and grouped so as to reflect different degrees of the chronic energy deficiency (CED) and obesity is shown at page 35 (James *et al.*, 1988).

Body Mass Index (BMI)

BMI	*Nutritional grade*
< 16.0	III degree CED
16.0 - 17.0	II degree CED
17.0 - 18.5	I degree CED
18.5 - 20.0	Low normal
20.0 - 25.0	Normal
25.0 - 30.0	Over weight (I degree obese)
> 30.0	Obese

Gomez Classification

The body weights and heights of preschool children were expressed as percentage of NCHS standards and their nutritional status was identified adapting Gomez classification given at page 35 (Gomez *et al.*, 1956).

Weight for age (% of standard)	*Nutritional grade*
> 90	Normal ('Normal' nutrition)
75 – 90	Grade I ('Mild' malnutrition)
60 – 75	Grade II ('Moderate' malnutrition)
< 60	Grade III 'Severe' malnutrition)

Clinical Assessment

Clinical assessment was conducted using structured and pretested schedule.

Statical Analysis

The analytical tools that were used in the study for the purpose of presentation, discussion and interpretation of the results was mostly that of time honoured tabular anaysis, besides simple statistical tools like means, percentages and standard deviations.

Two sample 'Z' test and paired 't' test were used to determine the significant difference between the two means (Snedecor and Cochran, 1967).

Test of significance of the difference between two "percentages" was calculated by using the formula given by Chandel (1993).

Concepts and Terms Used in the Study

The concepts and terms used in the study are as follows:

Household: A group of persons normally residing together and ordinarily taking food from the same kitchen.

Household members: A person whose stay is with the head of the family sharing the common kitchen.

Household size: Total number of members of the family who reside together sharing the same kitchen.

Nuclear family: Family comprising only husband, wife and children.

Joint family: Several nuclear families merged together and living under one roof sharing the kitchen.

Farm size: Small farm family refers to the operational holding area of < 5.00 acres of land, medium farm family refers to the operational land holding area of 5–10 acres of land, whereas large farm family refers to the operational holding area of more than 10 acres of land.

Landless Labourer: One who does not own any farm land, depends completely on labour for his livelihood.

Food security: Food security is defined as access by all people at all times to the food they need to live healthy lives (FAO, 1983).It is defined as physical and economic access to food to all children, women, and men at all times (Swaminathan, 1990).

Household Food Security: Household food security is defined as access to culturally acceptable food, that is adequate in terms of quantity and quality for all the household members (Gillespie and Masa, 1991). At the household level, food security is the ability of the household to secure enough food to ensure an adequate dietary intake for all of its members (Van Braun *et al.*, 1991).

Coping mechanisms: Adjustments made by the families to achieve food security.

Assets

a) ***Farm assets:*** Farm assets includes tractor, thresher engine, diesel engine, electric motor, bullock cart, connection of the well, chaff cutter, wooden plough, contour bunding, hand tools, fencing, seed drill, saw mill, oil expeller, flour mill, construction of new wells and deepening of wells.

b) ***Non-Farm assets*:** Non-farm assets include Ratio/Tape recorder, T.V., Bicycle, Motor cycle, Torch, fans, watches/clocks, small scale cottage industries, sewing machines, golden articles, silver articles, stainless steel articles, brass articles and furniture.

Reference period: The reference period for collection of data on all items of consumer expenditure is last month (30 days) preceding the month of enquiry.

Season: The results of the analysis are presented for two seasons i.e. "peak" and "lean" seasons. These two seasons are formed by grouping the data collected from two rounds of the study. The categories "peak" and "lean" are based on the availability of food from crop harvesting, which in turn depend on cropping patterns.

a) ***Peak season:*** The peak season is identified as the period from September to January, when Agricultural practices such as transplanting, weeding, harvesting and post harvest practices have to be taken up.

b) ***Lean season:*** The lean season is identified as March to July, when not much activity is found with women participation in production practices of the crops.

Household Consumer Expenditure

The expenditure incurred by a household on domestic consumption during the reference period is the household's consumer expenditure. The household's consumer expenditure is the total of the monetary values of consumption of various groups of items namely Food and Non-food items.

a) ***Food items:*** Included all the broad groups of items like cereals, milets, pulses, GLVs, roots & tubers, other vegetables, fruits, milk & milk products, livestock products including meat, fish, chicken & egg, sugar & jaggery, oil and nuts & oilseeds.

b) ***Non-food items:*** Included all the broad groups of items like clothing, bedding, shoes, electricity, fuel, house tax, education, entertainment, medicines, transport, tobacco & toddy, religious & social customs, cosmetics, soaps, tooth powder/ tooth paste, toys, other services like washerman, barber etc.

4

Results and Discussion

The results as emerged in the present study along with the analysis and discussion thereon constitutes the subject matter of this chapter. For effective understanding and clear exposition, it is discussed under the following major headings:

- — Village profiles
- — Socio-economic status of the families
- — Coping mechanisms adapted by the families for food security at household level in drought prone area
- — Food & nutrient intake of women and preschool children
- — Nutritional status of women and preschool children.

Village Profiles

The profiles of villages indicated that all the eight selected villages were similar in infrastructures such as roads, electricity, transport, medical, education, communication and other institutional facilities.

Socio-Economic Status of the Families

As far as the mean family size is concerned much difference was not noticed among large, medium, small farm and landless labour families. The mean family size was 5.6. It was slightly lower (5.3) in the case of large farm families as against landless labour families (5.8).

Type of Family

It is customary to classify the families into two categories viz., joint and nuclear. The findings indicated that 79 per cent of the families irrespective of occupation of farm acreage owned were of nuclear type, and only 21 per cent of the families were of joint type. The joint family systems appeared to be more prevalent among the large families.

Level of Education

It was observed that the level of education was directly proportionate to the land owned as well as economic status of the families.

The literacy level in the area was 38 per cent as against the state average of 44 per cent (NSS, 1991). The low level of education among the poor families could be attributed to poor financial condition and lack of awareness regarding the various facilities and concessions create for the benefit by the government. Further the analysis showed that majority of them were discontinuing the studies at the end of primary level and a few after secondary education. On an average only 0.3 per cent of the adult population reached graduation stage, indicating socio-economic backwardness of the area.

Housing

The results indicated that 98 per cent of the families were living in their own houses. On an average 108 families (36%) were living in masonry type of houses, 114 families (38%) were living in semi-masonry type of houses and 78 families (26%) were living in mud houses.

Sanitary Conditions

It was observed that the houses were poorly ventilated. The kitchen was dark and unhygienic in most of the houses. Garbage was collected daily, stored in backyard and used as manure for field. In all the eight selected villages, it was observed that there was no proper drainage facility. Waste water was freely flowing and in many places it was stagnant. Our of 300 families studied only 16 families (5%) were having toilet facility in their houses Public toilets provided in 3 villages out of the 8 villages.

Drinking Water Facility

Only 3(1%) families had water facility in their own house. The rest of the families had to fetch water from a distance. The distance from the houses to the water source was as follows:

Within 10 meters	-	53%
10–20 meters	-	30%
Above 20 meters	-	17%

The sources of drinking water were hand pumps (85%), wells (9%) and community or own taps (6%).

Other Facilities

Forty per cent of the families had electricity facility. Thirty nine per cent of the families owned transistors and four per cent of families owned Televisions. With regard to transport facilities, 10 per cent of families owned bullock carts, 23 per cent of families owned bicycles and only 6 per cent of families owned moped or motor cycles. The housing facilities and household appliances represented the general profiles of the families surveyed. Even though the houses were own environmental sanitation was very poor which calls for community action and education.

Coping Mechanisms Adapted by the Families for Food Security at Household Level in Drought Prone Area

The topic centered around the empirical examination of eight major groups of coping activities by the families for food security at household level. These included:

- Food production based coping mechanisms
    - i) Land based coping mechanisms
    - ii) Livestock based coping mechanisms
- Employment, Economic and Income generation based coping mechanisms
- Asset (Farm and Non-farm assets) based coping mechanisms
- Food procurement based coping mechanisms
- Food storage based coping mechanisms
- Food preparation, distribution and consumption based coping mechanisms
- Social based coping mechanisms
- Health based coping mechanisms

Food Production Based Coping Mechanisms

Land owned: Agricultural land forms the major fixed asset as it provides regular income and also carries the status in rural areas.

It was clear from the content of the Table 3 that on an average 6.68 acres per family of this drought prone area did not compare well with the state average of 16.25 acres per family (NSS, 1990-91).

i) Land based coping mechanisms:

Frequency distribution of the families according to the land based coping mechanisms adapted as incorporated in Table 4 and Fig. 3.

Table 4 indicated that an average of 94 per cent of families reported of shrinking net sown area during the study period. Seventy six per cent of the families were following intercrop adjustments of cropped area, with crop mixtures like groundnut & millet, groundnut + pulse and groundnut + other oil seeds (like gingelly, sunflower, etc.), to increase the production. The other land based coping mechanisms adapted were use of farm yard manure (100%), use of nitrogen fertilizers (80%), use of phosphorus fertilizers (48%), use of gypsum (35%), use of pesticides (40%) and use of weedicides (23%). Seed treatment procedures were followed by 62 per cent of families. Eighty four per cent of families reported of using hybrid or improved seeds. Nineteen per cent of families used canal or tank water and 16 per cent of families used well or bore well water for irrigation purpose. Only one per cent of the families used lift irrigation method. The per cent adaptation of land based coping mechanisms was directly proportionate to the land holding size (Fig. 3). Similar agricultural practices by the farming communities in dryland and drought prone areas have been reported by Richards (1983) in Mogbuama a village in Africa, Singh (1984), Agarwal (1992), Biman Basu (1992), Venkateswarlu (1992), Kalla *et al.* (1992) and Karanth (1993) in India.

ii) Livestock Based Coping Mechanisms

In order to quantify relative shifts in stocking rate of animals in peak and lean seasons, the data was classified according to six major animal species and the results are tabulated in Table 5. One of the most conspicuous adjustments to contain the impact of dry

Land Based Coping Mechanisms

1. Shrinking of sown area
2. Intercrop adjustments of cropped area
3. Use of Farm Yard Manure
4. Use of nitrogen fertilizer
5. Use of phosphorus fertilizers
6. Use of gypsum
7. Use of pesticides
8. Use of weedicides
9. Seed treatment methods followed
10. Use of hybrid/improved seeds

11a. Canal/tank

11b. Well/bore well (with or without motor)

11c. Lift irrigation

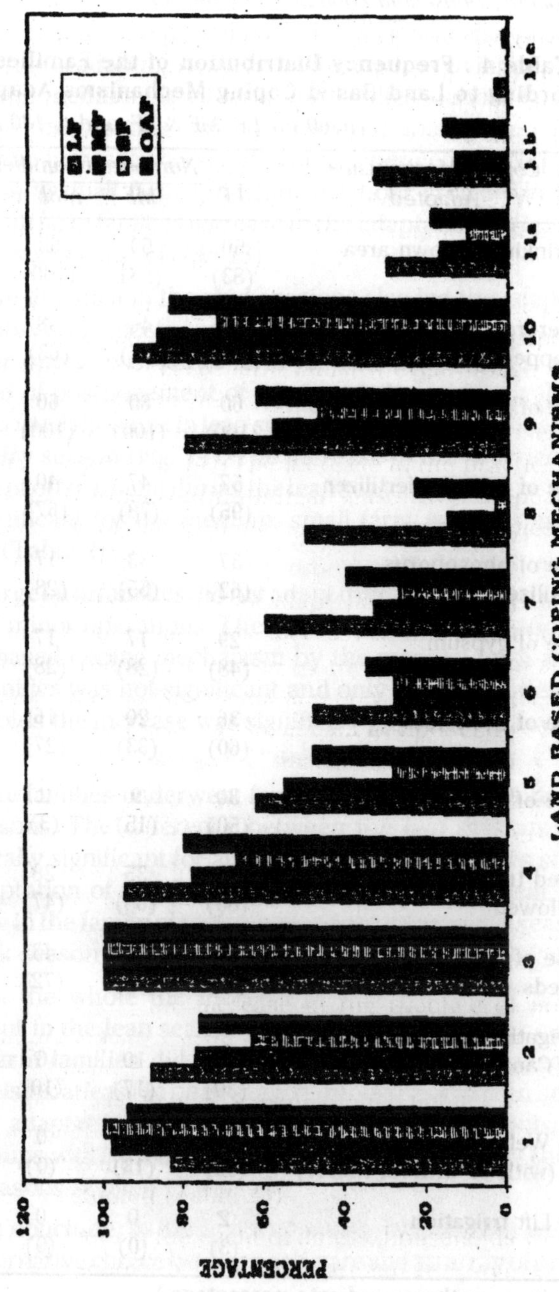

Fig. 3 : Distribution of Families According to Land Based Coping Mechanisms Adapted

Table 4 : Frequency Distribution of the Families According to Land Based Coping Mechanisms Adapted

(n=60 for LF, MF & SF; and n=180 for OAF)

S. No.	*Coping Mechanisms Adapted*	*Number of Families*			
		LF	*MF*	*SF*	*OAF*
1.	Shrinking of sown area	50 (83)	59 (98)	60 (100)	169 (94)
2.	Intercrop adjustments of cropped area	53 (88)	46 (77)	38 (63)	137 (76)
3.	Use of Farm Yard Manure	60 (100)	60 (100)	60 (100)	180 (100)
4.	Use of nitrogen fertilizer	57 (95)	47 (78)	40 (67)	144 (80)
5.	Use of phosphorus fertilizers	37 (62)	33 (55)	17 (28)	87 (48)
6.	Use of gypsum	29 (48)	17 (28)	17 (28)	63 (35)
7.	Use of pesticides	36 (60)	20 (33)	16 (27)	72 (40)
8.	Use of weedicides	30 (50)	9 (15)	2 (3)	41 (23)
9.	Seed treatment methods followed	48 (80)	35 (58)	28 (47)	111 (62)
10.	Use of hybrid/improved seeds	56 (93)	52 (87)	43 (72)	151 (84)
11.	Irrigation facilities used				
	a) Canal/tank	18 (30)	10 (17)	6 (10)	34 (19)
	b) Well/bore well (with or without motor)	20 (33)	8 (13)	0 (0)	28 (16)
	c) Lift irrigation	2 (3)	0 (0)	0 (0)	2 (1)

(Figures in parentheses indicate percentage.)

Table 5 : Average Number of Livestock Owned per Family

(n=60 for LF, MF & SF, n=120 for LL and N=300 for OAF)

S. No.	Livestock Particulars	Average number of livestock owned														
		Peak Season					Lean Season					'Z' Value				
		LF	*MF*	*SF*	*LL*	*OAF*	*LF*	*MF*	*SF*	*LL*	*OAF*	*LF*	*MF*	*SF*	*LL*	*OAF*
1.	Cows + buffaloes (milch)	6	2	2	1	3	7	1	1	0	3	0.93^{NS}	1.14^{NS}	1.12^{NS}	$3.87^{@}$	1.14^{NS}
2.	Calves	4	2	1	1	2	4	1	0	0	2	–	1.08^{NS}	1.89^{NS}	$3.52^{@}$	–
3.	Bullocks	3	2	2	1	2	3	1	1	0	1	–	0.92^{NS}	1.04^{NS}	3.17**	3.22**
4.	Dry animals	1	1	1	1	1	0	0	0	0	0	1.81^{NS}	1.44^{NS}	2.01*	3.36**	$3.56^{@}$
5.	Sheep/goats	8	9	23	25	16	2	2	8	11	6	$5.96^{@}$	$3.70^{@}$	$4.29^{@}$	$5.59^{@}$	$10.52^{@}$
6.	Poultry	4	3	4	6	4	3	2	2	3	3	0.61^{NS}	0.40^{NS}	1.44^{NS}	2.42*	1.27^{NS}

NS = Not significant; * = Significant at 5% level; ** = Significant at 1% level; @ = Significant at 0.1% level.

season lie in the reduction of the stocking rates of animals by the families. In landless labour families decline in mean number of all the species of animals during lean season was significant. In the small farm families the decline was significant for dry animals and sheep & goats, where as in large farm and medium farm families the decline was significant for only sheep & goats. The results revealed a universal decline in number of almost all animals during lean season except for milch cows/buffalows in large farm families. Muranjan (1991) also reported of reduction in stocking rates of animals in Maharashtra during lean period. The decline was mainly owing to death, selling, abandoning and gifting away. Abandonment of animals was a last resort of adaptation reported by the families during the lean season. Martha Alter Chen (1991) and Kalla *et al.* (1992) also reported of adaptation of similar livestock based mechanisms by the households in Gujarath and Rajasthan respectively.

The total availability of feed and fodder resources besides grains is generated from crop residues, common grazing lands, market purchases and non-market accruals on exchange basis. The demand for feed and fodder resources gets manifested in feeding animals, market sales, non-market exchanges and storing for augmenting future supply. In peak season most of the feed and fodder resources are farm produce but in lean season specially in dryland areas the feed and fodder supply was met mainly by relief and by purchases. It can be inferred that profound adverse effect upon augmentation of fodder and feed supplied for the maintenance of livestock holding in dry spells in lean season resulted in death or other form of disposal of animals by the families. The reduction in animal stocks was indirectly proportionate to the land holding size of the farming groups. This might be because of the common land property resources like grazing land, dry tank bed etc. were taken advantage of more by the bigger land owners than the small farm or landless labour households. Karanth (1993) also reported of the similar strategy adapted by the large farmers of Chitradurga district in Karnataka state.

Table 6 indicates the support received by the families from government for increasing food production. The support received by the families was indirectly proportionate to the land holding. On an average only 5.0 per cent of the families received subsidized

Table 6 : Frequency Distribution of the Families by Support Received from Government for Increasing Food Production

(n=60 for LF, MF & SF; and n=120 for LL and n=300 for OAF)

Sr. No.	*Support received (Supply of/ subsidies on)*	*Number of Families*				
		LF	*MF*	*SF*	*LL*	*OAF*
I.	**State Agriculture Department**					
	1. Groundnut seed	**–**	**6 (10)**	**9 (15)**	**–**	**15 (5)**
	2. Fertilizers (P.P. chemicals gypsum)	**–**	**18 (30)**	**22 (37)**	**–**	**'40 (13)**
II.	**State Veterinary Department**					
	1. Dairy Animals	**–**	**4 (7)**	**6 (10)**	**12 (10)**	**22 (7)**
	2. Sheep/Goat	**–**	**7 (12)**	**10 (17)**	**32 (27)**	**49 (16)**
	3. Fodder seeds like kokijonnalu, bajra, SIG-15 and mini kits from fodder development programmes	**4 (7)**	**5 (8)**	**13 (22)**	**–**	**22 (7)**

Figures within parentheses indicate percentage.

groundnut seed, 13 per cent of the families received fertilizers (PP chemicals and gypsum) from State Agricultural Department. None of the large farmers reported of receipt of support from the Agricultural Department. With regard to State Veterinary Department, 7 per cent of families received subsidies for dairy animals and 16 per cent of families received sheep or goats from the State Department. Seven per cent of families received kakijonnalu, bajra and minikits from fodder development programmes.

Even though the government provided support for increasing agriculture and livestock production, farmers were still following some hard options like shrinking of net sown area, selling of livestock etc., specially during dry spells of the lean season in these drought prone regions.

Employment, Economic and Income Generation Based Coping Mechanisms

Employment and Occupation

It was observed that about 43 types of activities were undertaken in peak and lean seasons by the families. Most often children specially girls were involved in home based trades like groundnut shelling, beedi making, tamarind peeling etc. In order to quantify relative shifts in occupational status of the selected family members in peak and lean seasons, the data was classified according to six major occupations and the differences in the occupational status of the families were analysed by category and presented in Table 7, Fig. 4. This analysis was undertaken as it serves as proxy for their earnings.

Regarding the occupational status of large farm families it was found that though the farm holding of these families was greater than 10 acres, they could not get necessary employment from their lands and still 12 per cent of families supplemented their main occupation by means of business or petty trades and traditional occupations like rug weaving, mat weaving, basket making etc., and 30 per cent of them were engaged in services during peak season. In the lean season, only 21 per cent of the family members got required employment from the land. Seventeen per cent of families supplemented their main occupation by means by traditional occupations followed by business and pettytrade (15%) and non-agricultural labour (9%). The decrease in farm occupation and increase in non-agricultural labour during lean season compared to peak season was significant at 0.1 per cent and 5 per cent levels respectively. With regard to agricultural labour, business & petty trade, service and traditional occupations, no significant difference was observed among large farm families between the two seasons (Table 7).

With regard to medium farm families, their main occupation during peak season was farming (86%) followed by traditional occupations (22%) services (22%), agricultural labour (18%), non-agricultural labour (12%) and business & petty trade (12%). During the lean season only 4 per cent of medium farm families got required employment from farming. The major occupation during lean season being traditional occupations (26%) followed by service (22%), non-agricultural labour (19%), business & petty trade (18%) and agricultural labour (10%). The decrease in farming activity of

Table 7 : Frequency Distribution of Families by Occupational Status

(n=144 for LF,n = 146 for MF, n=141 for SF, n=277 for LL and N=708 for OAF)

S.No. Occupation	Peak Season					Lean Season					'Z' Value				
	LF	MF	SF	LL	OAF	LF	MF	SF	LL	OAF	LF	MF	SF	LL	OAF
1. Farming	121 (84)	126 (86)	121 (86)	—	368 (52)	30 (21)	6 (4)	0	0	36 (5)	10.71@	14.09@	14.59@	—	19.59@
2. Agricultural labour	3 (2)	26 (18)	42 (30)	214 (77)	285 (40)	6 (4)	15 (10)	31 (22)	30 (11)	82 (12)	0.99NS	1.94NS	1.53NS	14.38@	12.00@
3. Non-Agricultural labour	4 (3)	18 (12)	26 (18)	69 (25)	117 (17)	13 (9)	28 (19)	58 (11)	141 (51)	240 (34)	2.14*	1.65NS	4.23@	6.30@	7.34@
4. Business/petty trade	17 (12)	18 (12)	23 916)	47 (17)	105 (15)	22 (15)	26 (18)	34 (24)	55 (20)	137 (19)	0.74NS	1.44NS	1.68NS	0.91NS	2.00*
5. Services	43 (30)	32 (22)	17 (12)	133 (48)	225 (32)	43 (30)	32 (22)	17 (12)	133 (48)	225 (32)	—	—	—	—	—
6. Traditional Occupations and others	17 (12)	32 (22)	21 (15)	33 (12)	103 (15)	24 (17)	38 (26)	25 (18)	39 (14)	126 (18)	1.21	0.80	0.68	0.70	1.52
7. Unemployed during lean season	–	–	–	–	–	38 (26)	58 (40)	52 (37)	101 (37)	249 (35)	–	–	–	–	–

(Figures within parenthesis indicate percentage.)
NS = Not significant; * = Significant at 5% level; ** = Significant at 1% level; @ = Significant at 0.1% level.

Occupations

1. Farming
2. Agricultural labour
3. Non-Agricultural labour
4. Business/petty trade
5. Services
6. Traditional occupations and others
7. Unemployed during lean season

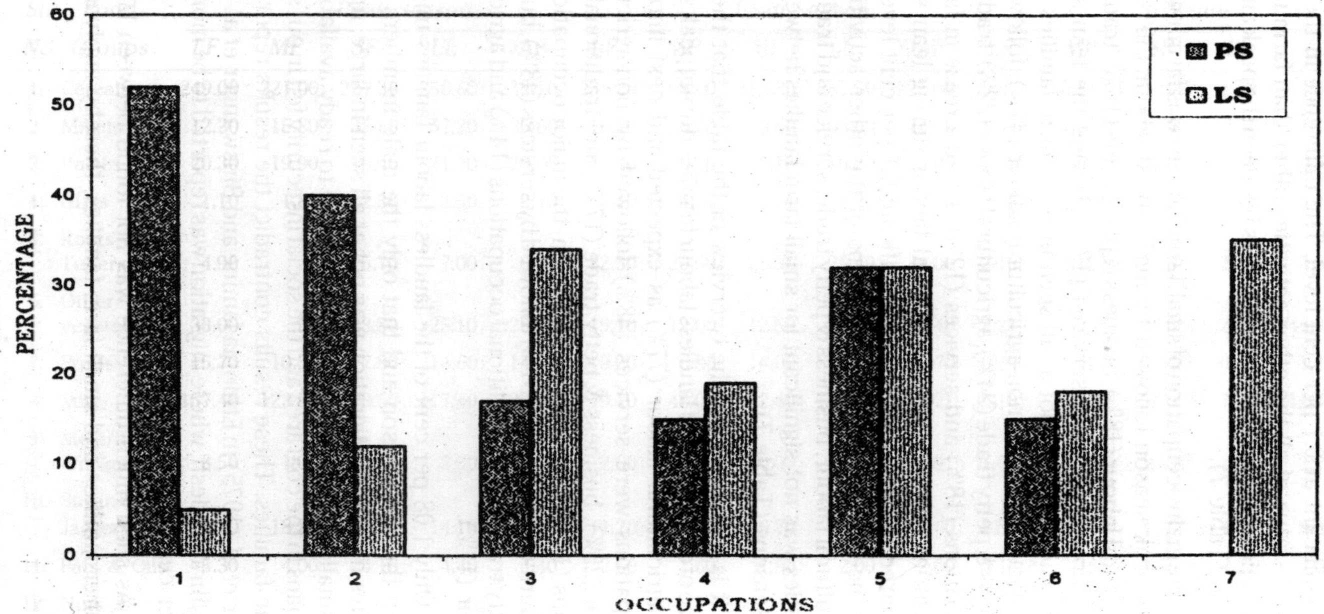

Fig. 4 : Distribution of Families According to Occupational Status

medium farm families during lean season compared to peak season was significant at 0.1 per cent level. The difference in the occupational status of all the other activities other than farming was not significant for medium farm families between the peak and lean seasons (Table 7).

The main occupation of small farm families was farming (86%) during peak season followed by agricultural labour (30%), non-agricultural labour (18%), business & petty trade (16%), traditional occupations (15%) and services (12%). During the lean season farming activity was not at all seen in small farm families as the main occupation was non-agricultural labour (41%), followed by business & petty trade (24%), agricultural labour (22%), traditional occupations (18%) and services (12%). The decrease in farming and the increase in non-agricultural labour during lean season compared to peak season was significant 0.1 per cent level. The difference in the occupational status of the other activities i.e. agricultural labour, business & petty trade, service and traditional activities was not significant for small farm families between the two seasons (Table 7).

It is obvious from the overview of the table that the main source of occupation of landless labour families during peak season was agricultural labour (77%) as expected and next important occupations were services (48%) followed by non-agricultural labour (25%), business & petty trade (17%), and traditional occupations (12%). During the lean season, the major occupation was non-agricultural labour (51%) followed by services (48%), business & petty trade (20%), traditional occupations (14%) and agriculture labour (11%).

Only 1.08 per cent of the landless labour families migrated during the lean season and that only the male members of the families migrated. Migration was not at all seen in large, medium and small farm families. This might be due to ready availability of the loans in the coal area and the social insecurity felt in out station by the families. These results contradict the results reported by Miller *et al.* (1975) in Ethiopia famine and Binswanger *et al.* (1984) in Andhra Pradesh, where migration was reported to be more than 40 per cent in drought prone areas.

As such much difference was not found between landless labourer families and small farm families, thereby implying that a small dryland holding area of 5 acres and less did not bring out much change in employment pattern.

The decrease in farm occupation and agricultural labour and increase in non-agricultural labour and business or petty trade during lean season was significant over the peak season (Fig. 4.). Reitsma *et al.* (1992) in Morocco, Kenya, Togo, Mexico and Spain and Karanth (1993) in Karnataka also reported to increase rate of non-agricultural labour works in the lean season.

Altogether in these lean parts 35 per cent of the people were unemployed during the lean season compared to peak season. The per cent of population unemployed were minimum in large farm group. Unemployed population were more in medium farm group than in small farm and landless labour group (Table 7). This might be due to the welfare and development programmes targeted by the government towards these low socio economic groups.

Hence, it hence be concluded that the cropping pattern intensity was very poor in the study area that the agriculture did not provide required employment opportunity to these families. Inspite of several welfare and development programmes initiated by the government, many families were underemployed.

Sources of Income

Since the income of families is the basic factor which determines the level of expenditure and savings, every effort was made to investigate it correctly. Per family annual income so arrived for the selected families is presented in Table 8 and Fig. 5.

From the critical examination of the Table 8 it was understood that the income in case of large families was Rs. 21,253 per family per year. The large farm families obtained maximum income from land (59%) followed by the livestock (22%), traditional occupations (10%), business or petty trade (7%) and labour (2%).

The annual income in case of medium farm families was of Rs. 11,519 per family. Out of this total income 37 per cent was derived from land followed by labour 21%), livestock (19%), traditional occupations (8%), business or petty trade (7%) and attached labour or house servant (7%). It is interesting to note that the medium farm families derived substantial amounts of income from labour though they have land indicating the socio-economic backwardness of this category of families in drought prone areas.

Income Sources

1. Land
2. Labour
3. Livestock
4. Business/petty trade
5. Attached labour/house servant
6. Traditional occupations

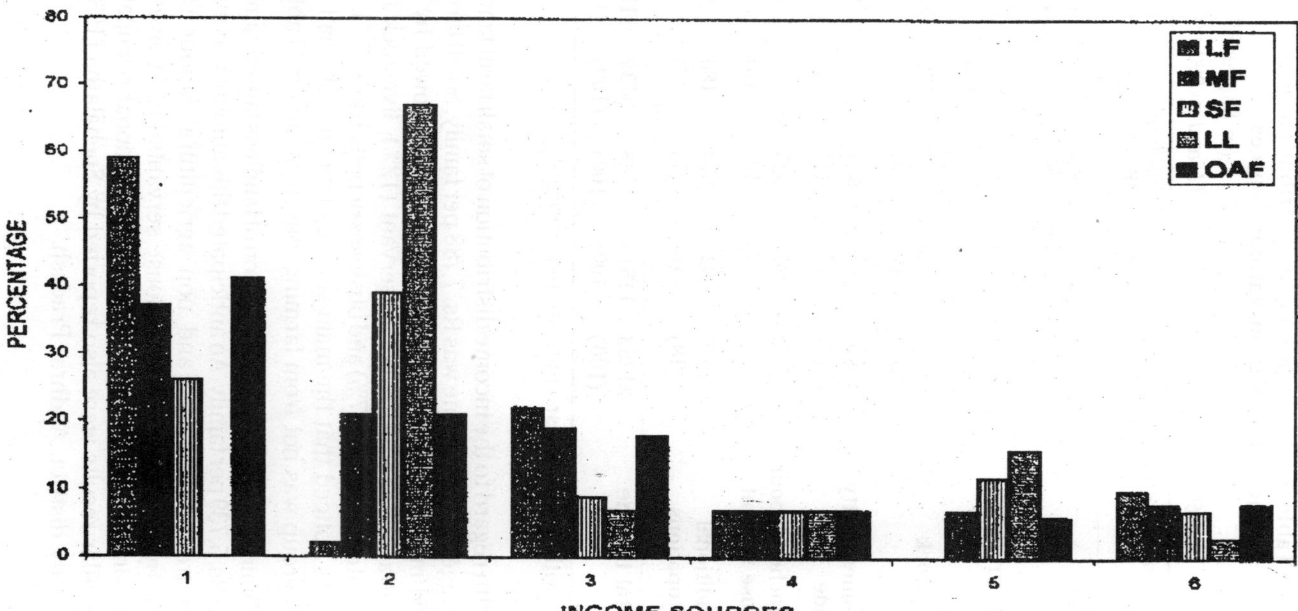

Fig. 5 : Distribution of Total Income by the Families from Various Sources

Table 8 : Average income distribution of the families from various sources

(in Rs./year/family)

(n=60 for LF, MF & SF; n=120 for LL and n=300 for OAF)

Sr. No.	*Income sources*	*Land holding*				
		LF	*MF*	*SF*	*LL*	*OAF*
I.	Land	12520 (59)	4282 (37)	2015 (26)	Nil	4704 (41)
2.	Labour	500 (2)	2450 (21)	3021 (39)	3814 (67)	2446 (21)
3.	Livestock	4722 (22)	2225 (19)	732 (9)	425 (7)	2026 (18)
4.	Business/Petty trade	1436 (7)	826 (7)	525 (7)	420 (7)	802 (7)
5.	Attached labour/ house servant	0	800 (7)	925 (12)	900 (16)	656 (6)
6.	Traditional occupations	2075 (10)	936 (8)	570 (7)	180 (3)	940 (8)
	Total income	**21253 (100)**	**11519 (100)**	**7788 (100)**	**5739 (100)**	**11574 (100)**

(Figures within parentheses indicate percentage.)

With regard to the income distribution of small farm families, the average annual income was Rs. 7,788 per family. Small farmers obtained maximum income from labour (39%) followed by land (26%), attached labour or house servant (12%), livestock (9%), traditional occupations (7%) and business or petty trade (7%). Here also it was noticed that the main source of income of small farm families group was not from farming, but from labour (Table 8).

Coming to the income distribution of landless labour families, it was of Rs. 5,739 per family. An anticipated this amount was mostly derived from agriculture and non agricultural labour (67%) followed by attached labour or house servants (16%), livestock (7%), business or petty trade (7%) and traditional occupations (3%). Similar results were also reported by Snehalatha (1988) in Rangareddy district, Andhra Pradesh.

Income from livestock formed some notable contribution to the total income of the families (Fig. 5). But when we look at the consumption of livestock products (Table 23 & 24) a pitiable condition was seen, wherein the subjects were selling the livestock products at the cost of consumption. It is, therefore, worthwhile to encourage not only this occupation but also to promote consumption of livestock products by the families.

Wage rates : The mean wage rates of the families is given in Table 9.

Table 9 : Mean wage rates of the families (in rupees)

Sr. No.	*Category*	*Mean wage (rate/day)*			
		Peak season	*Lean season*	*Difference*	*'Z'-value*
1.	Male	32±16 (6.53)	15±6 (2.45)	–17	42.22[@]
2.	Female	23±10 (4.08)	10±4 (1.63)	–13	51.25[@]
3.	Child	16±4 (1.63)	8±2 (0.82)	–8	75.94[@]

(Figures in parentheses indicate the S.D. values.)
@ = Significant at 0.1% level.

From the Table 9 the impact of dry spell on the mean wage rates of families could be readily seen. The mean wage rates were Rs. 32/-, Rs. 23/- and Rs. 16/- per male, female and child respectively during peak season, whereas the mean wage rates were only Rs. 15/-, Rs. 10/- and Rs. 8/- respectively for male, female and child during lean season. From the table it was quite evident that the difference in the mean wage rate was almost half and was highly significant at 0.1 per cent level between the seasons.

The wages paid in these dryland areas during lean season were lower which reduced the purchasing power even if people could get engaged in wage labour. Bindinger *et al.* (1990), Radha Krishna *et al.* (1991), Chandrasekhar Rao *et al.* (1992) and John McIntire (1981) also reported of the same results with regard to wage payments in lean periods in dryland and drought prone areas of Andhra Pradesh. As such minimum wages act was not followed in these areas.

Participation in Welfare Programmes

Several programmes have been implemented in these drought prone areas to sustain food production and also to increase income so that people can have access to marketed foods. The participation in welfare programmes (Employment and income generating activities of Government/voluntary organisations) by the families according to the category was analysed and tabulated in Table 10, and Fig. 6.

The percentage of participation in PDS was maximum (96%) by the families followed by ICDS (77%), DWCRA (33%), JRY (27%), RDT (11%) and YIP (7%).

Table 10 : Frequency Distribution of the Families by participation in welfare programmes (Employment/income generating activities of Government/ Voluntary Organisations)

(n=60 for LF, MF & SF; n=120 for LL and n=300 for OAF)

Sr. No.	Welfare Programmes	Number of Families				
		LF	MF	SF	LL	OAF
1.	PDS	50 (83)	58 (97)	60 (100)	120 (100)	288 (96)
2.	ICDS	29 (48)	39 (65)	46 (77)	117 (98)	231 (77)
3.	DWCRA	—	6 (10)	30 (50)	63 (53)	99 (33)
4.	JRY	2 (3)	6 (10)	12 (20)	60 (50)	80 (27)
5.	RDT	—	—	6 (10)	28 (23)	34 (11)
6.	YIP	—	3 (5)	5 (8)	13 (11)	21 (7)

(Figures within parentheses indicate percentage.)

The data presented in the Table 10 clearly indicated that the participation percentage of the families was indirectly proportionate to the income or to the and owned.

Several measures were undertaken by government of India and other voluntary organisations to provide food security to the

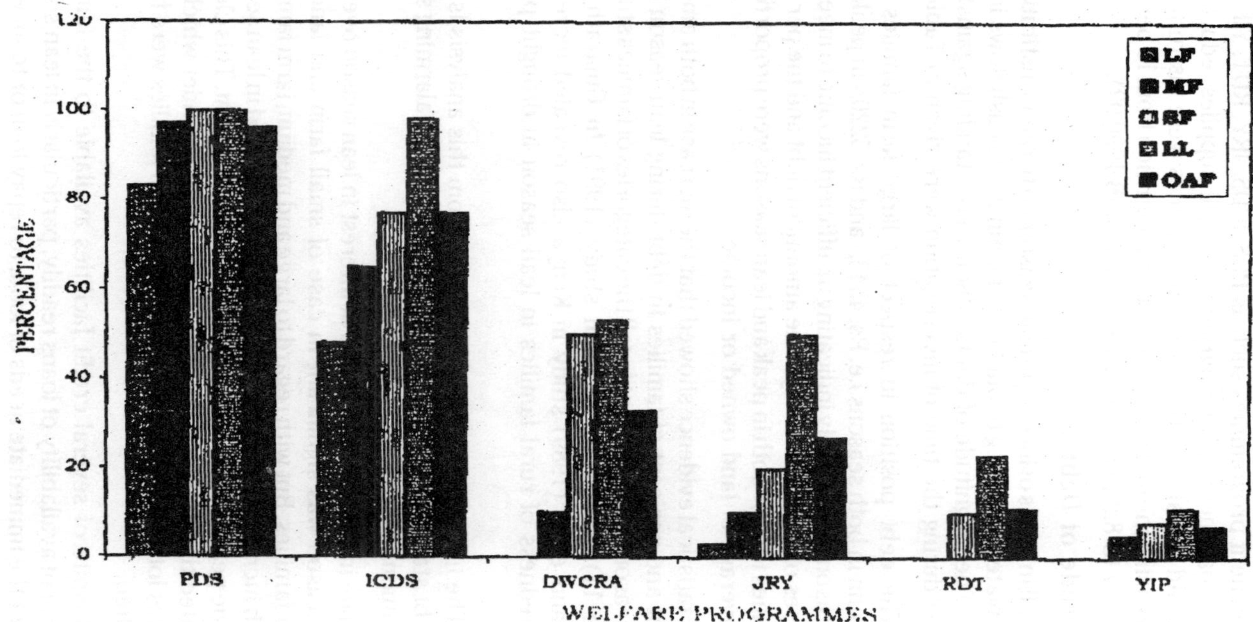

Fig. 6 : Per cent of Families Participated in Welfare Programmes

vulnerable sections of the society through number of welfare and development programmes such as PDS, ICDS, JRY, RDT, YIP etc.; in the departments of the agriculture, civil supplies, education, health and social welfare. These programmes were instrumental in decreasing the incidence of severe malnutrition from 15 per cent in 1975-79 to 8.9 per cent in 1990-92 (NNMB,1990-92).

Magnitude of Debts

Fall in levels of income in lean season led to rise in institutional and private borrowing to maintain the minimum cash flows in the family. The magnitude of debts which were standing against the families during the time of investigation were given in Table 11,

The debt position in respect of large farm families was maximum in both seasons i.e. Rs. 4543/- and Rs. 5220/- in peak and lean season respectively indicating insufficient income to meet the expenses of farm and family. The amount of debt and the per cent of families in debt both in peak and lean seasons were proportional with average of land owned or income.

Statistical evidence showed that the increase in both amount of debt and per cent of families in debt during lean season over peak season was significant for all the categories of families studied (Table 11). Martha Alter Chan study (1991) In Gujarath and Neumann *et al.* (1989) study in Kenya also revealed increased indebtedness of rural families in lean season in drought prone areas.

The inference that can be arrived from this analysis is that the debt status of the rural families has reached an alarming stage even among large farm families.

The increase in mean rate of interest in lean season over the peak season was significant in case of small farm and landless labour families. But with regard to large and medium farm families, though increase in the rate of interest was observed in lean season over the peak season, the increase was not significant. This clearly indicated the feebleness of economic conditions under which the helpless lot of landless labour and small farm families were being exploited.

Inspite of several credit facilities available to the families because of availability of loans readily, particularly in lean season to meet the immediate needs of food, to repay loan or to meet the

Table 11 : Magnitude of Debts of the Families

(n=60 for LF, MF & SF, n=120 for LL, n=300 for OAF)

S.No. Particulars	Peak Season					Lean Season					'Z' Value				
	LF	MF	SF	LL	OAF	LF	MF	SF	LL	OAF	LF	MF	SF	LL	OAF
1. Families who were in debt	4 (7)	33 (55)	36 (63)	96 (80)	171 (57)	14 (23)	46 (77)	50 (83)	120 (100)	230 (77)	2.45*	2.54*	2.47*	5.16@	5.21@
2. Average amount of debt per family (in Rs.)	4543 ±3922	3186 ±3374	2420 ±2696	906 ±300	2764 ±2219	5220 ±2596	4025 ±3746	3415 ±1394	2300 ±1864	3740 ±2948	2.73**	3.16**	6.19@	19.81@	11.23@
3. Average rate of interest (in Rs./ month/100 rupees)	1.00 ±1.00	1.00 ±1.00	1.44 ±0.12	1.60 ±0.80	1.26 ±1.48	2.40 ±0.49	2.58 ±0.84	3.04 ±0.78	3.40 ±0.49	2.86 ±1.34	0.9NS	0.63NS	15.86@	3.33@	37.21@

Figures in parenthesis indicate percentage

NS = Not significant; * = Significant at 5% level; ** = Significant at 1% level; @ = Significant at 0.1% level.

immediate needs of food, to repay loan or to meet the expenses of dowry or ceremonies, the families were taking loans from the money lenders, even though the rate of interest was high during the lean season.

Purpose of Indebtedness

The purpose of which the families took debts were categorised into eight major groups to quantify relative shifts of debt position in peak and lean seasons and tabulated in Table 12, and Fig. 7.

The rise in indebtedness of the families for medium and small farm and landless labour families during lean season over the peak season was mainly to meet the food needs and repay loans was significant (Table 12). Dowry or ceremonial expenses contributed to significant rise in indebtedness in all the four categories of families (Fig. 7).

The primary reason for the mounting debts which were beyond the repaying capacity was due to recurring and prolonged spells of droughts that slashed the area, over the years. As the area comes under dry farming zone and as the families have to depend entirely on rainfed agriculture, their income was affected severely. Consequently, they were forced to borrow continuously. Hence, the volume of indebtedness reached almost beyond their managerial abilities. This was because these debts were mostly raised from the private money lenders at exorbitant rate of interest.

Thus inspite of credit facilities almost every family was found to be in debts. Heavy borrowing was observed for performing marriages specially among small farm and landless labour households.

Food & Non-Food Expenditure

Food & non-food expenditure of the family is a function of the family income. The level and pattern of family expenditure mostly depends on many factors such as socio-economic status, customs, traditions and habits besides the family size and composition. In order to obtain a representative estimate on levels of living, the monthly expenditure of the four categories of families in peak and lean season were arrived based on the results of the investigation. The family expenditure pattern helps to estimate the standard of living during peak and lean seasons to seek policy formulations for economic development. The details regarding monthly expen-

Table 12 : Frequency Distribution of Families by Occupational Status

(n=144 for LF,n = 146 for MF, n=141 for SF, n=277 for LL and N=708 for OAF)

Sr. No.	Purpose of Indebtedness	Peak Season					Lean Season					'Z' Value				
		LF	MF	SF	LL	OAF	LF	MF	SF	LL	OAF	LF	MF	SF	LL	OAF
1.	Food	0	1 (2)	2 (3)	8 (7)	11 (4)	2 (3)	25 (42)	28 (47)	78 (65)	133 (44)	1.35^{NS}	$5.29^{@}$	$5.57^{@}$	$9.36^{@}$	$11.47^{@}$
2.	Health	2 (3)	3 (5)	3 (5)	7 (6)	15 (5)	1 (2)	1 (2)	1 (2)	2 (2)	5 (2)	0.35^{NS}	0.89^{NS}	0.89^{NS}	1.12^{NS}	2.00
3.	Construction	1 (2)	1 (2)	2 (3)	6 (5)	10 (3)	1 (2)	1 (2)	1 (2)	1 (1)	4 (1)	–	–	0.35^{NS}	1.82^{NS}	1.75^{NS}
4.	Dowry/ ceremonial	0	0	0	6 (5)	6 (2)	4 (7)	13 (22)	15 (25)	36 (30)	68 (23)	2.09*	$3.85^{@}$	$4.14^{@}$	$5.10^{@}$	$7.78^{@}$
5.	Consumer goods	0	2 (3)	2 (3)	2 (2)	6 (2)	2 (3)	4 (7)	1 (2)	1 (1)	8 (3)	1.35^{NS}	1.01^{NS}	0.35^{NS}	0.64^{NS}	0.78^{NS}
6.	Production	1 (2)	13 (22)	12 (20)	0	26 (9)	0	0	0	0	0	1.10^{NS}	$3.85^{N@}$	$3.65^{@}$	–	$5.32^{@}$
7.	Recurrent production equipment	0	1 (2)	1 (2)	0	2 (1)	2 (3)	2 (3)	1 (2)	0	5 (2)	1.35^{NS}	0.35^{NS}	–	–	1.01^{NS}
8.	Repay loan	0	14 (23)	16 (27)	67 (56)	97 (32)	0	2 (3)	3 (5)	2 (2)	7 (2)	–	3.26**	3.29**	$9.22^{@}$	$9.78^{@}$

(Figures within parenthesis indicate percentage.)
NS = Not significant; * = Significant at 5% level; ** = Significant at 1% level; @ = Significant at 0.1% level.

Purpose of Indebtedness

1. Food
2. Health
3. Construction
4. Dowry/ceremonial
5. Consumer goods
6. Production
7. Recurrent production equipment
8. Repay loan

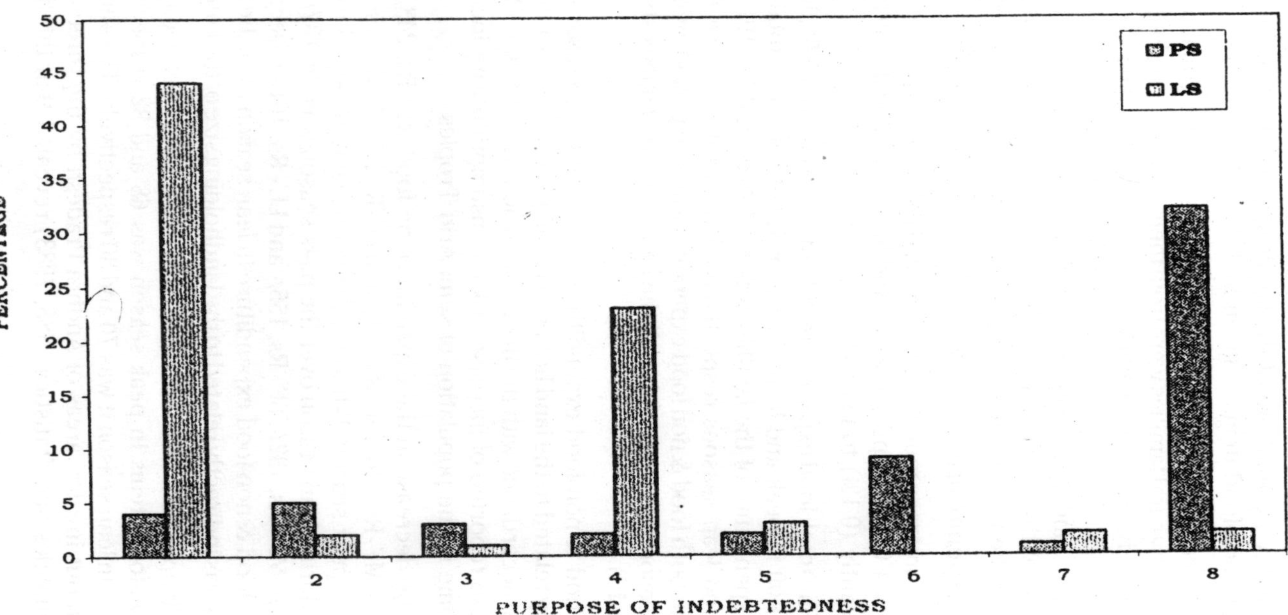

Fig. 7 : Distribution of Families According to Purpose of Indebtedness

diture per family according to category is given in Fig. 8a and 8b. The monthly expenditure of the families, separately for the total food and non-food items is given in Table 13.

The common sources for availability of the commodities consumed by rural families were from their own farm produce, kind wages, purchases in open market or fair price shop and gathered from farm or forest. The farm produced commodities, wages received in kind and the items gathered from farm or forest were evaluated at the market rates of these commodities in the villages, while for the purchased items, actual prices were considered.

Total Expenditure

The average monthly expenditure of the families were found to be Rs. 1,013.00 in peak season, and in lean season it decreased significantly (0.1%) to Rs. 632.00

The total food expenditure of the families was Rs. 684.00 and Rs. 441.00 in peak and lean seasons respectively. The total non-food expenditure of the families was Rs. 328.00 and Rs. 191.00 in peak and lean seasons respectively. Significant decrease (0.1% level) in both food & non food expenditure in lean period, over the peak season was observed in all the categories of families studied (Table 13).

Food & non food expenditure pattern in both seasons was directly related to the land holding size of the groups. The findings were in accordance with the findings of Thomas and James (1990) who also reported of increased food consumption with increase in income in the population of semi Arid Tropics.

The decrease in the expenditure on food was Rs. 243/- (LF Rs. 179/-, MF - Rs. 246/-, SF - Rs. 269/- and LL - Rs. 278/-) in lean season over the peak season. Whereas, the decrease in non-food expenditure during lean season over the peak season was Rs. 137/- (LF-Rs. 101/-, MF - Rs. 132/-, SF - Rs. 155/- and LL - Rs. 161/-). Decrease in both food & non-food expenditure in lean season over the peak season was indirectly related to the landholding size of the families.

The per cent distribution of total expenditure between food and non-food items in peak season was 68 and 32 respectively whereas in lean season it was 70 and 30 respectively. The surveys carried out in rural areas of Andhra Pradesh by the Directorate of Economics and Statistics (NSS, 1983) revealed that the distri-

Table 13 : Average monthly expenditure of the families (in Rs./family/month)

(n=60 for LF, MF, and SF, n=120 for LL and N=300 for OAF)

Sr. No.	Expenditure	Peak Season					Lean Season					'Z' Value				
		LF	MF	SF	LL	OAF	LF	MF	SF	LL	OAF	LF	MF	SF	LL	OAF
1.	Food Expenditure															
	Mean	885	696	619	537	684	706	450	350	259	441	11.92@	19.07	26.80	59.27@	42.82@
	S.D.	65.90	70.85	68.27	46.58	92.09	95.62	70.21	37.04	21.78	34.15					
	Percentage	63	69	70	71	68	63	72	76	80	70					
2.	Non-Food Exp.															
	Mean	514	309	266	224	328	413	177	111	63	191	7.95@	13.10@	35.57@	44.99@	47.37@
	S.D.	81.24	72.60	28.73	35.85	33.82	55.59	29.18	17.69	15.86	37.20					
	Percentage	37	31	30	29	32	37	28	24	20	30					
3.	Total Exp.															
	Mean	1399	1005	885	761	1013	1119	627	461	322	632	6.15@	14.71@	22.75@	34.27@	44.72@
	S.D.	296.51	151.82	134.92	125.31	134.33	190.36	128.62	51.09	63.06	60.14					
	Percentage	100	100	100	100	100	100	100	100	100	100					

@ = Significant at 0.1% level.

Food Items

1. Cereals
2. Millets
3. Pulses
4. Vegetables & Fruits
5. Milk
6. Fleshy foods
7. Edible oils
8. Nuts & Oilseeds
9. Sugar & Jaggery
10. Salt, spices and condiments
11. Beverages & others

Non-Food Items

1. Clothing, bedding and footwear
2. Electricity, fuel and housing
3. Durable goods, cosmetics, soaps, tooth paste, tooth powder etc.
4. Education
5. Transportation
6. Medicines
7. Pan, tobacco and intoxicants
8. Recreation
9. Others

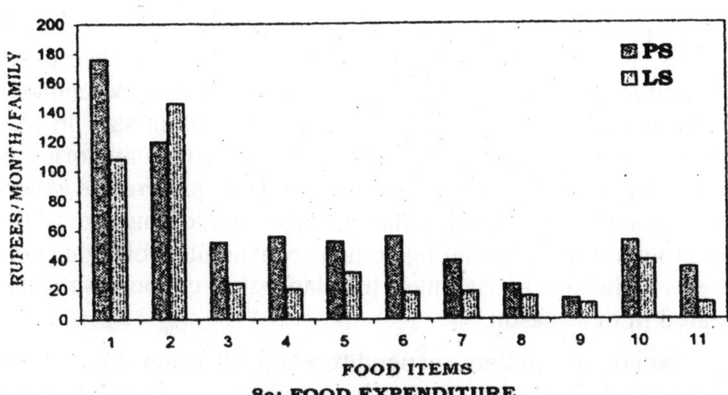

8a: FOOD EXPENDITURE

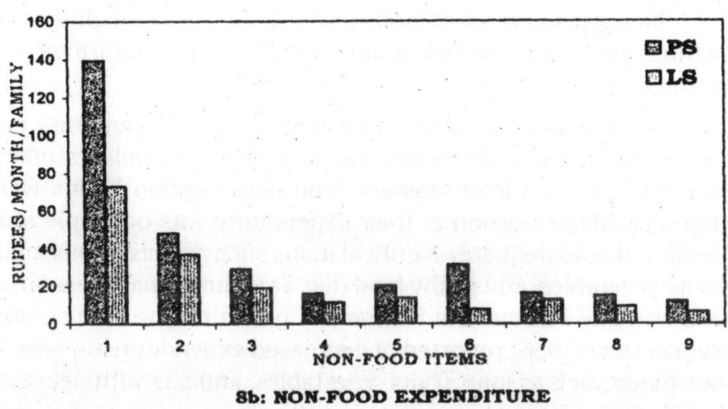

8b: NON-FOOD EXPENDITURE

Fig. 8 : Item-wise Expenditure Pattern of the Families

bution of expenditure between food & non-food items was 62 and 38 per cent respectively.

Food Expenditure

In peak season within food items, except landless labour families, all the other categories of families incurred highest expenditure on cereals. The trend indicated that the expenditure on cereals was directly related to the landholding size. In lean season, except large farm families, all the other categories of families incurred highest expenditure on millets. Here the expenditure trend was indirectly related to the landholding size of the four groups indicating shifting from the consumption of higher cost cereals to the lower cost millets to balance the economic shortage created in dry season.

Except for millets, expenditure on all other food items decreased significantly during lean season compared to peak season in all the categories of families studied.

The difference in expenditure pattern for all the food items, in all the four categories of families studied was highly significant at 0.1 per cent level in lean season over the peak season.

Increase in prices of foods during lean season might be one of the season for the drastic reduction in food expenditure pattern of the families.

An overview of these family consumption expenditure pattern clearly indicated that in all the categories of families studied, in both peak and lean seasons, food consumption habits were different. Major portion of their expenditure was on staple food items and not adequate on critical items such as pulses, oils, milk, fruits vegetables, and fleshy food (Fig. 8a). The primary reason for this was low income and increase in prices during lean season. Raman Devi (1986) reported of decreased expenditure on protective foods such as milk, fruits, vegetables, and fats with decrease in income.

The amount incurred towards the consumption of pulses in peak season was Rs. 52 per month per family and in lean season it was only Rs. 24 while the consumer expenditure towards pulses according to Directorate Survey (1983) was Rs. 33 in rural areas of Andhra Pradesh.

Non-food Expenditure

Among the monthly family expenditure on non-food items the first place was occupied by clothing, bedding and foot wear in both peak and lean seasons, except for the landless labour families in lean season. The landless labour families and small farmer families reported of purchasing clothing, bedding and foot were etc. in peak season immediately after crop harvesting as sufficient amount could be fetched in peak season after harvesting as a coping mechanism to withstand the economic stress created in lean season.

The expenditure on all the non-food items in lean season was lower compared to the peak season for all categories of families except for the expenditure on pan, tobacco and intoxicants for large farmers, the expenditure of which increased in lean season compared to peak seasons. This was because of the availability of the leisure time for large farmers in lean season, over peak season.

The expenditure on all the non-food items, for all the categories of the families studied in both peak and lean seasons were directly related to the landholding size, except for the medicines, the expenditure of which was indirectly related to the landholding size. This might be due to the intake of the poor quality food and maintenance of poor hygienic conditions by the medium, small farm and landless labour families over the large farm group.

The difference in the expenditure on all the non-food items in lean season for all the categories of families studied was highly significant over the peak season, except for recreation and other miscellaneous expenditure in the large farm group. The expenditure in large farm families decreased in lean season over peak season without any significance, indicating better living conditions of the large farm families over the other groups.

The expenditure on fuel, electricity and housing for all the four groups of families studied in both the seasons was very less. This was due to the fact that they depended on traditional fire wood available freely from the crop & animal wastes and from forest.

One important inference that can be drawn from this expenditure pattern on non-food items by all the categories of families in both the seasons is that very negligible amount was incurred on education which would provide necessary base for their future economic development (Fig. 8b).

The expenditure on non-food items by all the categories of families, in both seasons was very low, hence one can conclude that these families were leading subsistence level of living.

Studies conducted by Directorate of Economics and Statistics, Government of Andhra Pradesh (NSS, 1986) also indicated that 3/4th of the expenditure of the rural families was spent on essential food items only.

No doubt there was some change in the expenditure pattern on large farm families from those of other two classes of families in both peak and lean seasons but yet relatively, the low expenditure in monetary terms by the large farm families on certain essential items like education and on items which would given balanced diet were not much. Thus, there is a need to recognize the expenditure pattern even among these wealthy rural families so as to improve their economic aspects. The major source of income of these families was agriculture and agriculture labour and due to consequent droughts over the years these families income declined as already mentioned. The expenditure per family per month for both food & non food items in both seasons increased in monetary units with an increase in richness (Farm acreage). But as stated by Engel (1985) the per cent of the expenditure on food did not increase with an increase in farm size, but as a matter of fact it declined, from 71 per cent to 63 per cent and 80 per cent to 63 per cent in peak and lean season respectively.

One important inference that can be drawn is that the non-food expenditure was almost similar in respect of medium and small farm and landless labour families. The medium and small dry land holding of 10 and less acres practically did not have significant impact on expenditure pattern of these three categories of families.

Further, it is obvious from the critical examination of family consumer expenditure, that there was difference between peak and lean seasons, among the four categories of families along with imbalances between food and non-food items, and between essential and non-essential items. Even the expenditure on important items, which were essential from the point of balanced diet, education and durable assets was negligible (Fig. 8a & 8b). As such much scope lies to reorganize the family expenditure patterns among rural families, particularly in lean season which would help to bring in the needed change to have good health and to improve their economic conditions.

Economic Based Coping Mechanisms

The altered source-wise income composition of the families, in lean season made them adapt themselves to work on non-agricultural business, accepting to work for low wages, almost half to that of peak season wages, increase in employing children for borrowing money, increase in call for remittances from parents and relatives, increase in foraging in common property, postponement of acquisition of all consumer durables and resulted in a hard option of even taking loans or begging of either grains or money (Table 14 and Fig. 9).

A total of 34 per cent of families accepted to work for low wages almost half that of peak season wages, in lean season by taking activities which consume more energy and less returns (Fig. 9). Bidinger *et al.* (1990) in Dokur, a drought prone village in the semiarid Telangana region of Andhra Pradesh, Radhakrishna *et al.* (1991) in dry zones of Andhra Pradesh, and Chandrasekhara Rao *et al.* (1992) in Prasakam district of Andhra Pradesh also reported the same. It was observed that about 43 types of income generating activities were undertaken in lean season by the families.

Increase in employing children for borrowing money in lean season among landless labour families was significant at 1 per cent level. The large farm, medium farm and small farm families did not adapt this coping strategy of employing children for borrowing money (Table 14).

Increase in call for remittance from parents and relatives in lean season by the all four categories of families was significant. This practice was also followed by large farm families in lean season (7%) which was not at all seen in peak season. Similar observations were also made by Richards (1983) in Mugbuama village in Africa.

The practice of foraging in common properly lands showed significant increase for all the categories of families studied during lean season (Table 14). Karanth (1993) also observed the same practice by the farmers in lean season in Karnataka.

Another economic coping mechanism followed by the four categories of families in lean season over the peak was postponement of acquisition of all consumer durables (89%) and decrease

Table 14 : Frequency Distribution of Families according to Economic Coping Mechanisms Adapted

(n=60 for LF, MF, & SF, n=120 for LL, n=300 for OAF)

Sr. No.	Coping Mechanism	Peak Season					Lean Season					'Z' Value				
		LF	MF	SF	LL	OAF	LF	MF	SF	LL	OAF	LF	MF	SF	LL	OAF
1.	Accepting to work for low wages (almost half to that of peak season wages) in lean season	–	–	–	–	–	6 (10)	13 (22)	26 (43)	56 (47)	101 (34)	2.51^{*}	$3.85^{@}$	$5.73^{@}$	$8.59^{@}$	$11.09^{@}$
2.	Employing children for borrowing money	–	–	3 (5)	10 (8)	13 (4)	–	–	6 (10)	24 (20)	30 (10)	–	–	1.04^{NS}	2.68^{**}	2.88^{**}
3.	Accepting remittances from parents and relatives	–	1 (2)	3 (5)	7 (6)	11 (4)	4 (7)	20 (33)	29 (48)	67 (56)	120 (40)	2.09^{*}	$4.47^{@}$	$5.34^{@}$	$8.37^{@}$	$10.64^{@}$
4.	Foraging in common property	7 (12)	8 (13)	10 (17)	20 (17)	45 (15)	20 (33)	18 (30)	21 (35)	38 (32)	97 (32)	2.75^{**}	2.27^{*}	2.25^{*}	2.70^{**}	$4.91^{@}$
5.	Postponement of acquisition of all consumer durables in lean season	–	–	–	–	–	35 (58)	56 (93)	57 (95)	120 (100)	268 (89)	$7.00^{@}$	$10.21^{@}$	$10.42^{@}$	$15.49^{@}$	$21.93^{@}$

Contd.....

Table 14 : (Contd.)

(n=60 for LF, MF, & SF, n=120 for LL, n=300 for OAF)

S.No. Coping Mechanism	Peak Season					Lean Season					'Z' Value				
	LF	MF	SF	LL	OAF	LF	MF	SF	LL	OAF	LF	MF	SF	LL	OAF
6. Curtailment in the expenditure on all food & non-food items	–	–	–	–	–	60 (100)	60 (100)	60 (100)	120 (100)	300 (100)	$10.95^{@}$	$10.95^{@}$	$10.95^{@}$	$15.49^{@}$	$24.49^{@}$
7. Taking loans (grain)	–	–	–	–	–	–	–	3 (5)	10 (8)	13 (4)	–	–	1.75^{NS}	3.16**	$3.50^{@}$
8. Begging (grain/ money)	–	–	–	–	–	–	–	1 (2)	2 (2)	3 (1)	–	–	1.10^{NS}	1.56^{NS}	1.74^{NS}

(Figures within parenthesis indicate percentage.)

NS = Not significant; * = Significant at 5% level; ** = Significant at 1% level; @ = Significant at 0.1% level.

Economic Coping Mechanisms

1. Accepting to work for low wages (almost half to that of peak season wages) in lean season.
2. Employing children for borrowing money.
3. Accepting remittances from parents and relatives.
4. Foraging in common property.
5. Postponement of acquisition of all consumer durables in lean season.
6. Curtailment in the expenditure on all food and non-food items.
7. Taking loans (grains).

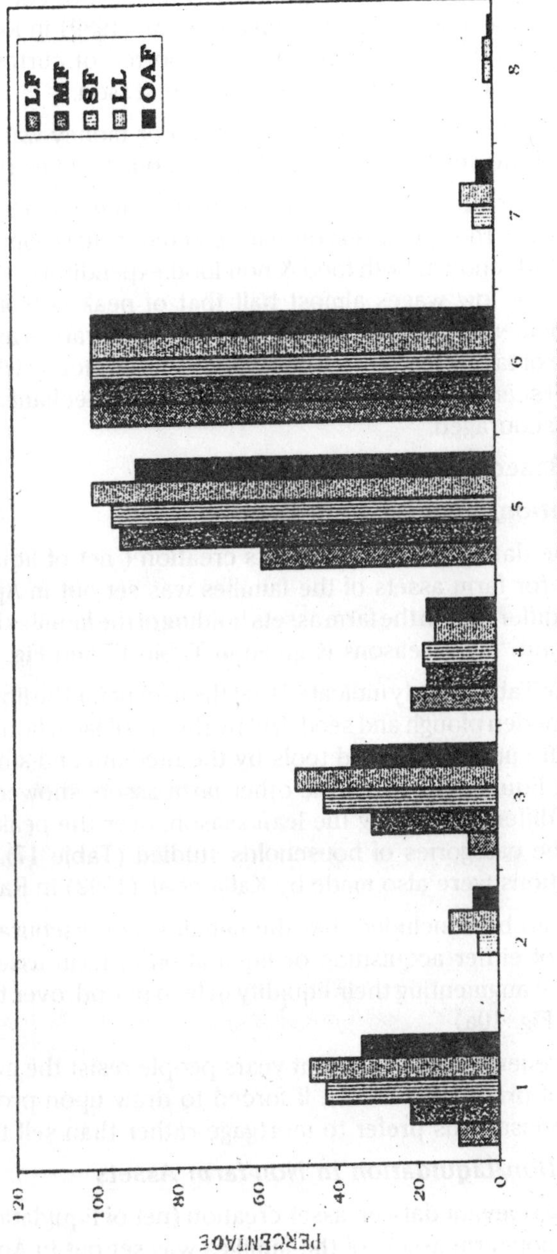

Fig. 9 : Distribution of Families according to Economic based Coping Mechanisms Adapted

in food & non-food expenditure (100%) for cost of consumption shortfalls, for food security. neumann *et al.* (1989) in Kenya and Kalla *et al.* (1992) in Rajasthan also reported of curtailment in acquisition of consumer durables in lean season.

Borrowing and begging either grain or money was also followed by the small farm and landless labour families (Fig. 9).

The drastic reduction in occupation and income in lean season over the peak season has resulted in hard options like drastic reduction in both food & non-food expenditure, accepting to work for low wages almost half that of peak season wages, postponement of acquisition of all consumer durables and in the practice of taking loans & even begging grain or money which was not at all seen in peak season (Table 14). These mechanisms need to be discouraged.

Asset Based Coping Mechanisms

Acquisition/Liquidation in Farm Assets

The data pertaining to assets creation (net of liquidation) process for farm assets of the families was set out in Appendix-VII. The difference in the farm assets holding of the families between "peak" and "lean" seasons is given in Table 15 and Fig. 10a.

The Table clearly indicated that the except for the liquidation of the wooden plough and seed drill by the small farm households, and chaff cutters and hand tools by the medium and small farm families, liquidations of all the other farm assets showed on significant difference during the lean season, over the peak season for all the categories of households studied (Table 17). Similar observations were also made by Kalla *et al.* (1992) in Rajasthan.

It can be concluded that the families had discouraged the activity of either acquisition or liquidation of farm assets, as a method of augmenting their liquidity in lean period, over the peak season (Fig. 10a)

In general even in drought years people resist the mortgage or sale of productive assets. If forced to draw upon productive assets, households prefer to mortgage rather than sell them.

Acquisition/Liquidation in Non-farm Assets

The relevant data on asset creation (net of liquidation) process for non-farm assets of the families was set out in Appendix-

Table 15 : Frequency Distribution of Families according to Acquisition/Liquidation of Farm Assets

(n=60 for LF, MF, & SF, n=120 for LL, n=300 for OAF)

Sr. No.	Particulars Mechanism	Number of families											
		Peak Season				Lean Season				'Z' Value			
		LF	MF	SF	OAF	LF	MF	SF	OAF	LF	MF	SF	OAF
1.	Tractor	8 (13)	–	–	8 (4)	7 (12)	–	–	7 (4)	0.17^{NS}	—	—	—
2.	Thrasher engine/Diesel engine/ Electric motor/connection of the well	13 (22)	2 (3)	–	15 (8)	12 (20)	1 (2)	–	13 (7)	0.27^{NS}	0.35^{NS}	–	0.36
3.	Bullock cart	20 (33)	7 (12)	3 (5)	30 (17)	20 (33)	7 (12)	3 (5)	30 (17)	–	–	–	–
4.	Construction of new wells/ hand pumps	3 (5)	1 (2)	–	4 (2)	4 (7)	1 (2)	–	5 (3)	0.46^{NS}	–	–	0.61^{NS}
5.	Deepening of wells	4 (7)	2 (3)	–	6 (3)	6 (10)	3 (5)	–	9 (5)	0.59^{NS}	0.56^{NS}	–	0.97^{NS}
6.	Contoor bunding/fencing	4 (7)	3 (5)	2 (3)	9 (5)	4 (7)	3 (5)	2 (3)	9 (5)	–	–	–	–
7.	Wooden plough/seed drill	55 (92)	40 (67)	20 (33)	115 (64)	52 (87)	33 (55)	10 (17)	95 (53)	0.89^{NS}	1.35^{NS}	2.02*	2.12*
8.	Chaff cutter/hand tools	60 (100)	60 (100)	60 (100)	180 (100)	59 (98)	54 (90)	45 (75)	158 (88)	1.10^{NS}	2.51*	4.14@	4.79@
9.	Saw mill/oil expeller/flour mill	2 (3)	1 (2)	–	3 (2)	2 (3)	1 (2)	–	3 (2)	–	–	–	–

Farm Assets

1. Tractor
2. Thresher engine/Diesel enginge/Electric motor/connection of the well
3. Bullock cart
4. Construction of new wells/hand pumps
5. Deepening of wells
6. Contoor bunding/fencing
7. Wooden plough/seed drill
8. Chaff cutter/hand tools
9. Saw mill/oil expeller/flour mill

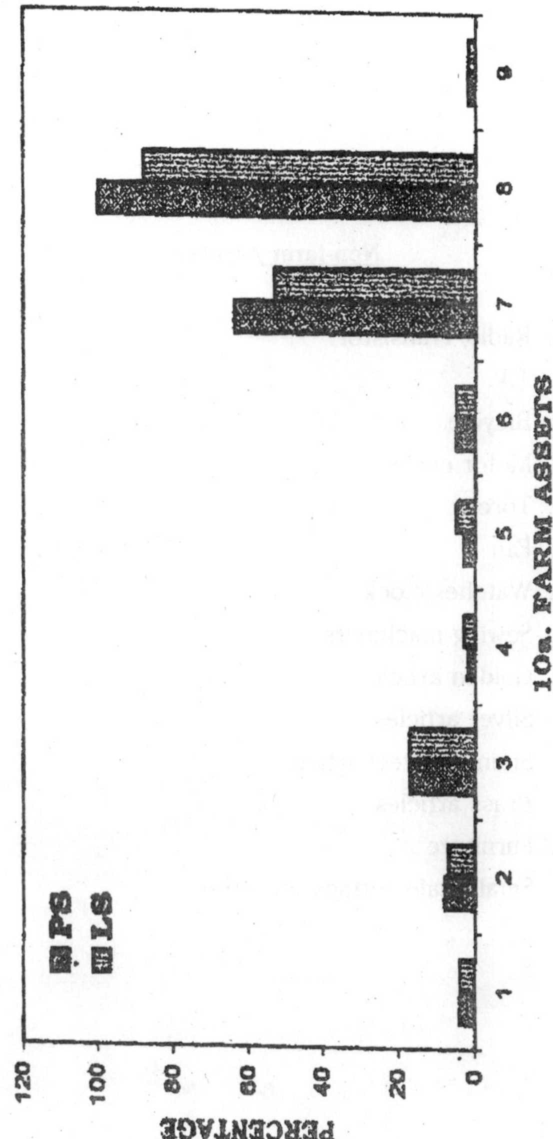

Fig. 10 : Distribution of Families according to Acquisition/Liquidation of Assets

Non-farm Assets

1. Radio/Transistor
2. T.V.
3. Bicycle
4. Motor cycle
5. Torch
6. Fan
7. Watches/clock
8. Sewing machiners
9. Golden articles
10. Silver articles
11. Stainless steel articles
12. Brass articles
13. Furniture
14. Small-scale cottage industries.

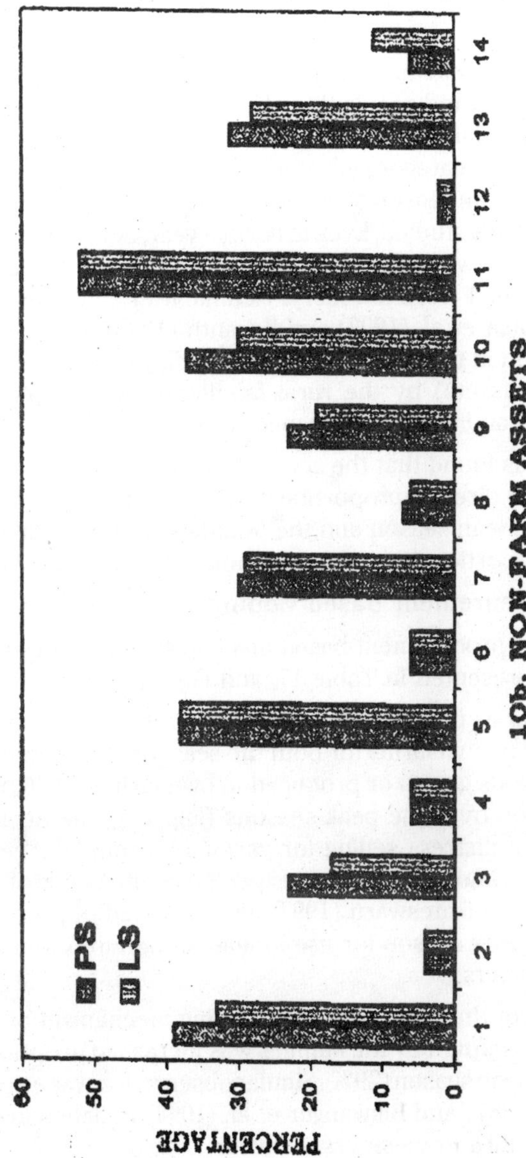

Fig. 10 : Distribution of Families according to Acquisition/Liquidation of Assets

VIII. The difference in non-farm asset holding of the families between peak season and lean season is given in Table 16, and Fig. 10b.

It was found that except for liquidation of radio or transistor, silver articles and acquisition of small scale cottage industries by the landless labour households, the acquisition or liquidation of all the other categorised non-farm assets were not significant during the lean season over the peak season, for all the categories of households studied. Even in normal year, non-productive assets were often pawned as security for loans. The most common items to be pawned were jewellery. Neumann *et al.* (1989), Muraujan (1991), Kalla *et al.* (1992) and Karanth (1993) also observed the same trend in the acquisition and liquidation of assets (farm and non-farm assets) by the rural families in Kenya, Maharashtra, Rajasthan and Karnataka respectively.

It was found that the acquisition of both farm and non-farm assets was directly proportionate to the land holding size of the families in lean season and the liquidation of the same was indirectly proportionate to the land holding size (Table 16).

Food Procurement Based Coping Mechanisms

Food procurement based mechanisms adapted by the families are presented in Table 17, and Fig. 11.

As far as possible the families, procured the foods grown or produced in own farms for both the seasons. The decrease in the various foods grown or produced in own farm was 66 per cent in lean season over the peak seasons (Fig. 11). The decrease was because of distress selling for various reasons like ceremonial, repay loans and to meet the unexpected health needs of the family members. Venkateswaru (1992) also reported of procuring food grains in peak season for use in lean season in Andhra Pradesh by the farmers.

One of the other identified coping mechanism of food procurement adapted by the families was increased in opting to work for kind in lean season (29%). Similar observation was also reported by John (1981) and Biswanger *et al.* (1994) in Sahelian countries and in Andhra Pradesh respectively.

Drastic decrease in the various sources of income of the families resulted in decrease in purchasing foods by paying cash (38%), decrease in procuring food grains through PDS (55%) and

Table 16 : Frequency Distribution of Families according to Acquisition/Liquidation of Non-farm Assets

(n=60 for LF, MF, & SF, n=120 for LL, n=300 for OAF)

S. No.	Coping Mechanism	Number of families: Peak Season LF	MF	SF	LL	OAF	Lean Season LF	MF	SF	LL	OAF	'Z' Value LF	MF	SF	LL	OAF
1.	Radio/ Translator	48 (80)	32 (53)	16 (27)	20 (17)	116 (39)	48 (80)	30 (50)	11 (18)	10 (8)	99 (33)	–	0.33^{NS}	1.18^{NS}	2.11*	1.53^{NS}
2.	T.V.	10 (17)	3 (5)	–	–	13 (4)	10 (17)	2 (3)	–	–	12 (4)	–	0.56^{NS}	–	–	–
3.	Bicycle	18 (30)	16 (27)	13 (22)	22 (18)	69 (23)	17 (28)	12 (20)	9 (15)	13 (11)	51 (17)	0.24^{NS}	0.90	0.99	1.4^{NS}	1.84^{NS}
4.	Motor Cycle	15 (25)	3 (5)	–	–	18 (6)	15 (25)	3 (5)	–	–	18 (6)	–	–	–	–	–
5.	Torch	43 (72)	26 (43)	18 (30)	26 (22)	113 (38)	43 (72)	26 (43)	18 (30)	26 (22)	113 (38)	–	–	–	–	–
6.	Fan	12 (20)	6 (10)	–	–	18 (6)	12 (20)	6 (10)	–	–	18 (6)	–	–	–	–	–
7.	Watches/ clock	56 (93)	22 (37)	6 (10)	6 (5)	90 (30)	56 (93)	22 (37)	5 (8)	3 (3)	86 (29)	–	–	0.38^{NS}	0.79^{NS}	0.27^{NS}
8.	Sewing machines	8 (13)	6 (10)	2 (3)	4 (3)	20 (7)	8 (13)	6 (10)	1 (2)	2 (2)	17 (6)	–	–	0.35^{NS}	0.50^{NS}	0.47^{NS}

Contd....

Table 16 : (Contd.)

Sr.	Coping	Number of families										'Z' Value				
		Peak Season					Lean Season									
No.	Mechanism	LF	MF	SF	LL	OAF	LF	MF	SF	LL	OAF	LF	MF	SF	LL	OAF
9.	Golden articles	41 (68)	12 (20)	6 (10)	10 (8)	69 (23)	40 (67)	9 (15)	3 (5)	4 (3)	56 (19)	0.12^{NS}	0.72^{NS}	1.04^{NS}	1.70^{NS}	1.20^{NS}
10.	Silver articles	56 (93)	23 (38)	12 (20)	21 (18)	112 (37)	55 (92)	19 (32)	6 (10)	9 (8)	89 (30)	0.21^{NS}	0.69^{NS}	1.53^{NS}	2.30*	1.82^{NS}
11.	Stainless steel articles	52 (87)	41 (68)	23 (38)	41 (34)	157 (52)	52 (87)	41 (68)	23 (38)	41 (34)	157 (52)	–	–	–	–	–
12.	Brass articles	4 (7)	3 (5)	0 (0)	0 (0)	7 (2)	4 (7)	3 (5)	0 (0)	0 (0)	7 (2)	–	–	–	–	–
13.	Furniture	52 (87)	23 (38)	6 (10)	11 (9)	92 (31)	52 (87)	22 (37)	4 (7)	7 (6)	85 (28)	–	0.11^{NS}	0.59^{NS}	0.88^{NS}	0.81^{NS}
14.	Small scale cottage industries	9 (15)	6 (10)	3 (5)	1 (1)	19 (6)	10 (17)	8 (13)	7 (12)	9 (8)	34 (11)	0.30^{NS}	0.52^{NS}	1.37^{NS}	2.62^{NS}	2.20^{NS}

(Figures within parenthesis indicates percentage.)
NS = Not significant; * = Significant at 5% level; @ = Significant at 0.1% level

increase in purchasing food grains on loan or credit (4%).

It was surprising to note that there was drastic decrease in procuring grain through PDS in lean season specially with regard to medium, small farm and landless labour families. In peak season 96 per cent of families procured grains through PDS, whereas in lean season only 41 per cent of families reported of procuring grain through PDS. As far as large farm families were considered the decrease in procurement of grains from PDS in lean season over peak season was not significant. This could be attributed to the economic access to purchase staple food grains by the large farm families. But with regard to the other categories of families, i.e. medium farm, small farm and landless families, the decrease in procurement of grain through PDS during lean season over the peak season was significant at 0.1% level (Table 17), indicating the feeble condition of these poor families to purchase food grains through PDS in lean season even through they were supplied on subsidiary rates.

The other important food procurement mechanisms adapted by the families in lean season for food security were (Table 19) increase in sending children to Anganwadi centres (22%), procuring cheaper quality grains (36%), increase in collecting forest produce for food and generation of income (52%) and increase in procuring unconventional foods like tubers, wild green leafy vegetables, mushrooms, whitants (Odontoterms obesus), rabbits etc. (9%).

Irvine (1952), Becker (1983), Richards (1983), FAO (1983), May *et al.* (1985) and Neela *et al.* (1994) also reported of eating forest foods such as wild roots & tubers, fruits, seeds, beans, green leafy vegetables and mushrooms etc. in lean season to suppress hunger; in Africa, Senegal, Mugbuana, India, Northern Brazil and India respectively. The difference in the food procurement based mechanisms adapted by the families was indirectly proportionate to the landholding size.

It can be concluded that the major food procurement mechanisms adapted by the families in lean season included procuring the foods grown on produced in the own farms, decrease in purchasing foods by paying cash and decrease in purchasing PDS ration, increase in opting to work for kind than cash, purchasing food grains on loan or credit increase in sending children to AWC,

Table 17 : Frequency Distribution of Families according to Food Procurement Coping Mechanisms Adapted

(n=60 for LF, MF, & SF, n=120 for LL, n=300 for OAF)

S.No. Coping Mechanism	Peak Season					Lean Season					'Z' Value				
	LF	*MF*	*SF*	*LL*	*OAF*	*LF*	*MF*	*SF*	*LL*	*OAF*	*LF*	*MF*	*SF*	*LL*	*OAF*
1. Procuring the foods grown or produced from own farms	60 (100)	60 (100)	60 (100)	NA	180 (100)	30 (50)	21 (35)	10 (17)	NA	61 (34)	6.32@	7.60@	9.23@	–	13.32@
2. Opting to work for kind than cash	2 (3)	6 (10)	9 (15)	26 (22)	43 (14)	2 (3)	20 (33)	31 (52)	76 (63)	129 (43)	–	3.07**	4.29@	6.42@	7.87@
3. Purchasing foods by paying cash (from wholesale shops/retail shops/local farmers/weekly shandy days)	60 (100)	60 (100)	60 (100)	120 (100)	300 (100)	54 (90)	44 (73)	30 (50)	57 (48)	185 (62)	2.51*	4.33@	6.32@	9.18@	11.86@
4. Purchasing food grains on loan/ credit	6 (10)	10 (17)	14 (23)	31 926)	61 (20)	6 (10)	10 (17)	17 (28)	41 (34)	74 (25)	–	–	0.63^{NS}	1.35^{NS}	1.4^{NS}
5. Sending children to AVC	18 (30)	27 (45)	33 (55)	87 (73)	165 (55)	29 (48)	39 (65)	46 (77)	117 (98)	231 (77)	2.02*	2.20*	2.24*	5.50@	5.00@

(Contd.)

Table 17 : (Contd.)

S.No. Coping Mechanism	Peak Season LF	MF	SF	LL	OAF	Lean Season LF	MF	SF	LL	OAF	'Z' Value LF	MF	SF	LL	OAF
6. Sending children to AWC	18	27	33	87	165	29	39	46	117	231	2.02*	2.20*	2.24*	$5.50^{@}$	$5.00^{@}$
7. Procuring cheaper quality grains	4 (7)	7 (12)	14 (23)	32 (27)	57 (19)	12 (20)	27 (45)	40 (67)	85 (71)	164 (55)	2.08*	$4.00^{@}$	$4.84^{@}$	$6.82^{@}$	$5.13^{@}$
8. Collecting forest produce for food & generation of income	2 (3)	5 (8)	8 (13)	19 (16)	34 (11)	9 (15)	18 (30)	49 (82)	113 (94)	189 (63)	2.30*	3.07**	$7.57^{@}$	$12.14^{@}$	$13.19^{@}$
9. Procuring unconventional foods like tubers, wild green leafy vegetables, mushrooms, white ants, rabbits, etc.	2 (3)	5 (8)	7 (12)	16 (13)	30 (10)	2 (3)	10 (17)	13 (22)	32 (27)	57 (19)	–	1.49^{NS}	1.46^{NS}	2.71**	3.13*

(Figures within parenthesis indicate percentage.)

NS = Not significant; * = Significant at 5% level; ** = Significant at 1% level; @ = Significant at 0.1% level.

Food Procurement Based Mechanisms

1. Procuring the foods grown or produced from own farms.
2. Opting to work for kind than cash.
3. Purchasing foods by paying cash (from wholesale shops/retail shops/local farmers/weekly shandy days).
4. Purchasing food grains on loan/credit.
5. Procuring grain through PDS.
6. Sending children to AWC.
7. Procuring cheaper quality grains.
8. Collecting forest produce for food & generation of income.
9. Procuring unconventional foods like tubers, wild green leafy vegetables, mushrooms, white ants, rabbits, etc.

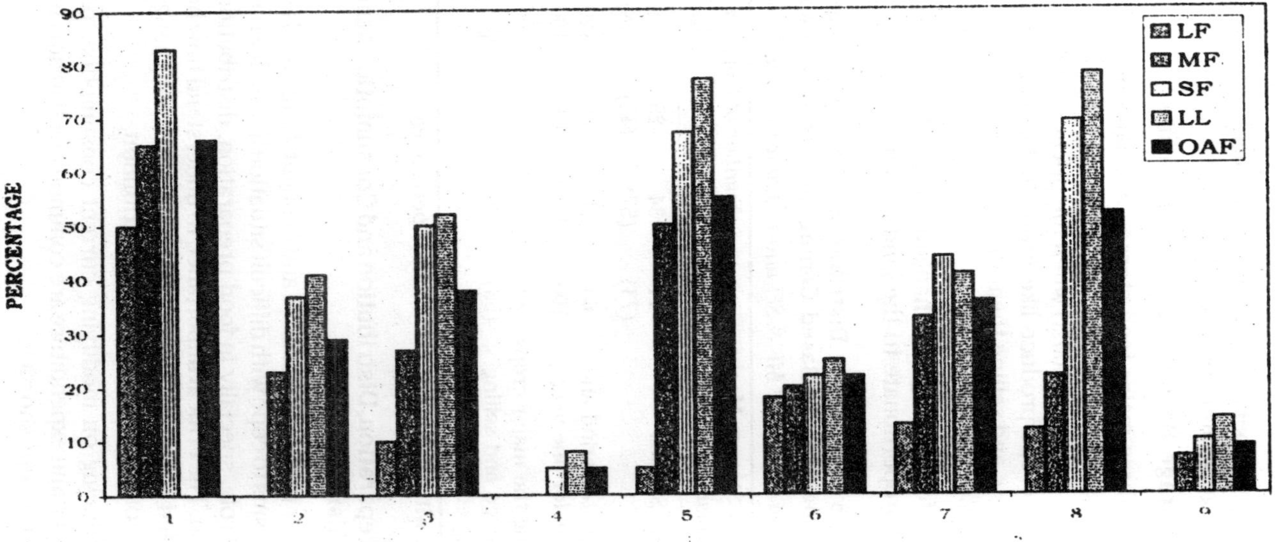

Fig. 11 : Distribution of Families According to Food Procurement Based Coping Mechanisms Adapted

procuring cheaper quality grains, and collecting forest produce for food and generation of income.

Food Storage Based Coping Mechanisms

The three major food storage mechanisms adapted by the families were storing staples (46%) and storing tamarind and chillies for one year (100%) when the prices were low and storing the major crops produce like groundnuts, sunflower seeds and other millets and selling them during economic crises for higher prices (18%) (Table 18).

The food storage mechanisms adapted by the families were directly proportionate to the land holding size.

Table 18 : Frequency Distribution of Families According to Food Storage Based Coping Mechanisms Adapted

(n=60 for LF, MF & SF; and n=120 for LL and n=300 for OAF)

Sl. No.	*Food Storage Mechanisms Adapted*	*Number of Families*				
		LF	*MF*	*SF*	*LL*	*OAF*
I.	Storing Staples	44 (73)	34 (57)	25 (42)	34 (28)	137 (46)
2.	Storing tamarind and chillies for one year	60 (100)	60 (100)	60 (100)	120 (100)	300 (100)
3.	Storing the major crops produced and selling during economic crisis	32 (53)	17 (28)	6 (10)	0 (0)	55 (18)

(Figures within parentheses indicate percentage.)

Food Preparation, Distribution and Consumption based Coping Mechanisms

Over the years of famine and drought, households developed mechanisms to cope with difficult situation in which women played a major role, specially in food preparation, distribution and consumption. The critical importance to understand how households responded to the drought is an examination of changes in food preparation, consumption and distribution.

Reducing on modifying current consumption, particularly food intake and expenditure are common mechanisms to deal with uncertainty and shortage.

The results of estimates of consumption i.e. adjustments made in time of mortgagees to meet food needs are presented in Table 19 and Fig. 12.

Table 18 : Frequency Distribution of Families According to Food Storage Based Coping Mechanisms Adapted

(n=60 for LF, MF & SF; and n=120 for LL and n=300 for OAF)

Sl. No.	Adjustments made during food shortages	Number of Families				
		LF	*MF*	*SF*	*LL*	*OAF*
1.	Curtailment in number of meals from 3 to 2 in a day because of					
	a) Economic reasons	1 (17)	29 (48)	35 (61)	83 (70)	148 (63)
	b) No time to eat because of heavy work load	–	4 (7)	2 (4)	–	6 (2)
	c) Do not like to eat three times/less work	5 (8)	23 (38)	20 (33)	35 (29)	83 (28)
	Total	6 (10)	56 (93)	57 (95)	118 (98)	237 (79)
2.	Reducing meal size	4 (7)	56 (93)	57 (95)	120 (100)	237 (79)
3.	Cooking only once in a day	20 (33)	29 (48)	37 (62)	86 (72)	172 (57)
4.	Substitution of millets to rice, horsegram or cowpea to redgram	6 (10)	17 (28)	46 (77)	106 (88)	175 (58)
5.	Curtailment in consumption of protective foods	4 (7)	57 (95)	58 (97)	118 (98)	237 (79)
6.	Curtailment in consumption of coffee and tea	9 (15)	20 (33)	43 (72)	95 (79)	167 (56)
7.	Diluting the milk/or giving coffee/tea instead of milk to the children	5 (8)	13 (22)	37 (62)	86 (72)	141 (47)
8.	Changing meal pattern with chutnies and other available bulk foods	1 (2)	13 (22)	30 (50)	71 (59)	115 (38)

Contd

Table 18 : (Contd.)

Sl. No.	Adjustments made during food shortages	Number of Families LF	MF	SF	LL	OAF
9.	Eating the grain kept for seed purpose	2 (3)	10 (17)	12 (20)	NA	24 (13)
10.	Use of more puffed rice	–	16 (27)	19 (32)	42 (35)	77 (26)
11.	Curtailing work and activities to supress hunger	0	2 (3)	5 (8)	13 (11)	20 (7)
12.	Forceful starvation	0	3 (5)	4 (7)	9 98)	16 (5)

(Figures within parentheses indicate percentage.)

Coping Mechanisms

1. Curtailment in number of meals from 3 to 2 in a day.
2. Reducing meal size.
3. Cooking only once in a day.
4. Substitution of millets to rice, horsegram or cowpea to redgram.
5. Curtailment in consumption of protective foods.
6. Curtailment in consumption of coffee and tea.
7. Diluting the milk/or giving coffee/tea instead of milk to the children.
8. Changing meal pattern with chutnies and other available bulk foods.
9. Eating the grain kept for seed purpose.
10. Use of more puffed rice.
11. Curtailing work and activities to supress hunger.
12. Forceful starvation.

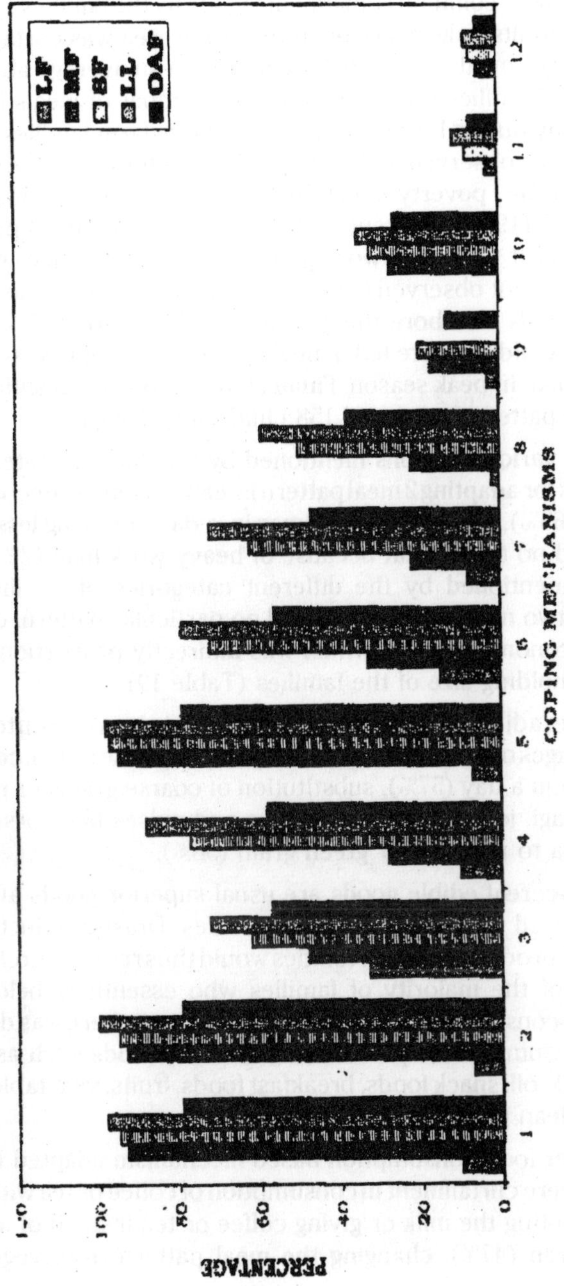

Fig. 12 : Distribution of Families According to Food Preparation, Consumption and Distribution Based Coping Mechanisms Adapted

The most common adjustments made by the families specially by the adults in lean season in the study area was curtailment in number of meals from 3 to 2 in a day. On an average about 79 per cent of families reported of shifting number of meals from 3 to 2 in a day during lean season. Even in large farm families (10%) this shift was observed, indicating the stern shortages during dry spells and the poverty situation in these drought prone areas. Webb *et al.* (1992) also reported of shifting to one meal per day in Ethiopia. It was note worthy that gender difference in food sharing was not observed in the study area. Even the male heads of households also bore the greatest burden of food shortages. However, children were fed 3 meals per day during lean seasons usual i.e. like in peak season. Finau (1985), reported of shifting to one meal pattern in 4 out of 158 children in Tonga.

The various reasons mentioned by the different categories of families for adapting 2 meal pattern in lean season were economic reasons (63%), not like to eat 3 times in a day or having less work (28%) and no time to eat because of heavy work load (2%). The reasons mentioned by the different categories of families for adapting two meal pattern followed no particular pattern, except for the economic reason, which was indirectly proportionate to the land holding size of the families (Table 19).

Other adjustments made by the families in lean season to meet the shortages of food needs were reducing meal size (79%), cooking only once in a day (57%), substitution of coarse grains or millets such as ragi, jowar, bajra etc. to rice and pulses like horsegram or cowpea to redgram or green gram (58%).

Non-cereal edible goods are usual superior goods and are characterised by high demand elasticities. Drastic reduction in income or production opportunities would thus reduce purchasing capacity of the majority of families who essentially belong to producer-consumer group. As scarcity worsens, there was decline in the consumption of protective and costly foods such as flesh foods, milk, oil, snack foods, breakfast foods, fruits, vegetables etc. (79%) in lean period by the families.

Other food consumption based mechanism adapted by the families were curtailment in consumption of coffee or tea with milk (56%), diluting the milk or giving coffee or tea instead of milk to the children (47%), changing the meal pattern from vegetable curries and dhal preparations to more dilute foods such as chutneys with foods available at home or eating with salt or chillies or onions or butter milk or *korivikaram*, a red chilli preparation (38%); use of more puffed rice in place of co-centered snack foods or cereal for preschool children to kill appetite (26%), curtailing work and activities to suppress hunger (7%) and even under going starvation (5%) to void purchasing food during the lean period which posed a severe financial burden for most households (Table 21). Finau (1985) reported that 11 preschool children out of 158 suffered from hunger during slack periods in Tonga.

The adjustments made by the families in food preparation, consumption and distribution in times of shortages to meet food needs showed an indirect relationship to the landholding size (Fig. 12). However, certain practices like use of more puffed rise to kill the appetite in preschool children, curtailing work and activities to suppress hunger and undergoing starvation were not observed among large farm households.

From the data recorded it could be inferred that despite availability of cereals at subsidized price, the erosion in income generating capacity of the families resulted in sizable reduction in purchase of non-cereal consumer articles. Some families even reported of eating seeds during the severe food crisis that normally would have been reserved for planting. The variety of foods consumed was highly limited to cereal + millet groundnut, tamarind and chillies.

Social Based Coping Mechanisms

A variety of evidence points, reported by the families, with regard to the sociai based adjustments are represented in Table 20, and Fig. 13.

Dry spells in the regions represent the extreme and of the spectrum in terms of food crisis. They also pose in the most stark terms the socio-economic conditions relating to the intra-household food sharing and provide a minimum intra-family relations. However, in the present study, 42 per cent of households reported of no change in the family relations i.e. the intra family relations were normal during lean season. Fifty eight per cent of families indicated disturbed family relations during lean season over the peak season. The lean season has resulted in disturbed family

Table 20 : Frequency Distribution of Families According to Social Based Coping Mechanisms Adapted

(n=60 for LF, MF & SF; and n=120 for LL and n=300 for OAF)

Sl. No.	*Social based coping mechanisms adapted*	*Number of Families*				
		LF	*MF*	*SF*	*LL*	*OAF*
I.	Change in family relations					
	a) Normal/No change	57 (95)	30 (50)	14 (23)	26 (22)	127 (42)
	b) Slightly disturbed	3 (5)	25 (42)	23 (38)	46 (38)	97 (32)
	c) Disturbed	0	5 (8)	7 (12)	20 (17)	32 (11)
	d) Extremely disturbed	0	0	16 (27)	28 (23)	44 (15)
2.	Curtailment in the use of intoxicants, cigarettes and pan in lean season	21 (35)	26 (43)	29 (48)	58 (48)	134 (45)
3.	Postponement of all family functions other than marriages	3 (5)	8 (13)	9 (15)	20 (17)	40 (13)
4.	Sending children to grand parents house or sending daughter-in-law alongwith; children to parents house.	2 (3)	7 (12)	13 (22)	26 (22)	48 (16)
5.	Postponement/avoiding travel or travelling by walk	3 (5)	11 (18)	15 (25)	38 (32)	67 (22)
6.	Curtailment of recreation like cinema	3 (5)	12 (20)	15 (25)	30 (25)	60 (20)
7.	Curtailment of guests/ relatives/friends/gifts/ beggers	4 (7)	10 (17)	32 (53)	94 (78)	140 (47)
8.	Maintaining the secrecy of food resources in the forests	0	1 (2)	7 (12)	28 (23)	36 912)

(Figures within parentheses indicate percentage.)

relations specially among small farm and landless labour lot of poor. Reduced socialization was also reported by Webb *et al.* (1992) in Ethiopia.

Curtailment in the use of intoxicants, cigarettes and pan in lean season, over the peak season was reported by 45 per cent of the families (Table 22). However, there were also some cases, specially in large farm families who reported of increased use of intoxicants, cigarettes and pan because of the increased availability of leisure time in lean season compared to peak season.

The other methods reported for coping with dry spell were of postponement of all family functions other than marriages (13%), sending children to grand parents house or sending daughter-in-law along with children to parents house (16%), postponement or avoiding travel or traveling by walk (22%), curtailment of recreation like cinema (20%) and avoiding guests or relatives or friends or gifts or beggars (47%). The disturbance in social activities was indirectly proportionate to the land holded by the families. Martha Alter Chen (1991) reported that in Gujarath in peak season caste neighbors frequently made small loans or gifts to one another. But in slack seasons these reciprocal or charitable transactions were narrowed from caste neighbours to kinship network.

Maintaining the secrecy of food resources in the forests during lean season was reported by the medium and small farm and landless labour households. Twelve per cent of the families reported of the maintaining the secrecy of the food resources in the forests (Fig. 13).

It can be conclude that all social activities involving expenditure got considerably reduced minimizing social arena of life cycle itself, giving rise to life at low equilibrium of living to let the dry spell periods pass.

4.3.8. Health Based Coping Mechanisms

In order to qualify the relative shifts in choosing the various health facilities available in peak and lean seasons, the data was classified into twelve major providers and the results are given in Table 21 and Fig. 14.

The results indicated that private medical care was the predominant choice for health care in both seasons for all the categories of families studied. The decrease in the availment of

Social Based Coping Mechanisms

1. Change in family relations
   a) Normal/No Change
   b) Disturbed
2. Curtailment in the use of intoxicants, cigarettes and pan in lean season.
3. Postponment of all family functions other than marreiages.
4. Sending children to grand parents house or sending daughter-in-law along with children to parents house
5. Postponement/avoiding travel or travelling by walk
6. Curtailment of recreation like cinema.
7. Curtailment of guests/relatives/friends/gifts/beggars
8. Maintaining the secrecy of food resources in the forests.

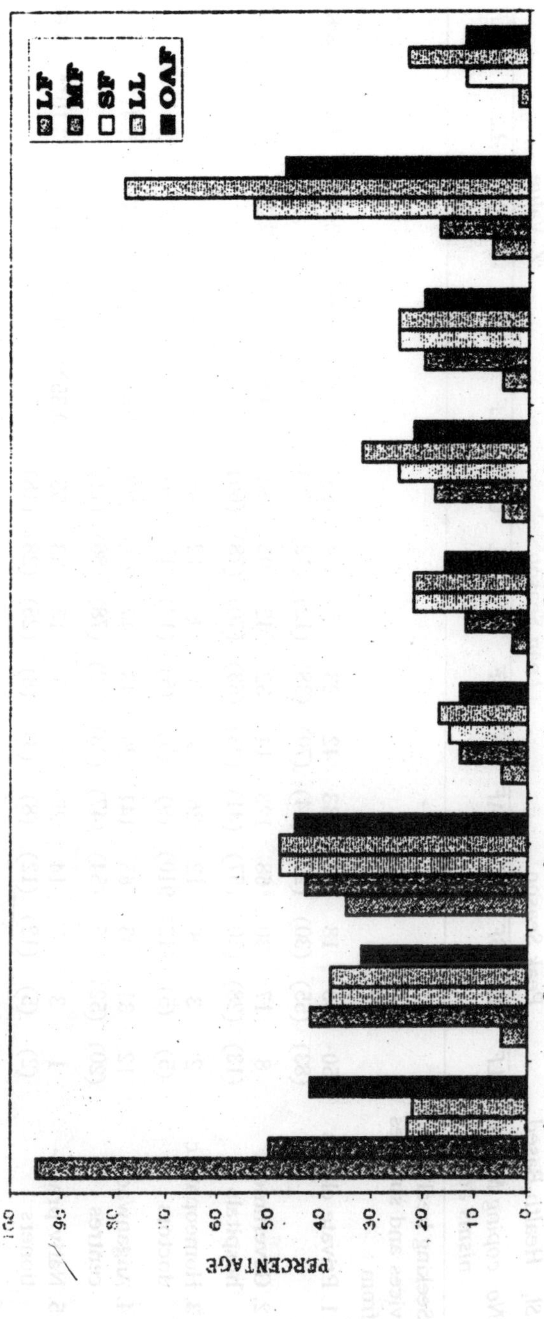

Fig. 13 : Distribution of Families According to Social Based Coping Mechanisms Adapted

Table 21 : Frequency Distribution of Families according to Health based Coping Mechanisms Adapted

(n=60 for LF, MF, & SF, n=120 for LL, n=300 for OAF)

Sl. No.	Health Based coping Mechanisms adapted	Number of families										'Z' Value				
		Peak Season					Lean Season									
		LF	MF	SF	LL	OAF	LF	MF	SF	LL	OAF	LF	MF	SF	LL	OAF
	Seeking health services and supplies from :															
1.	Private clinics	50 (83)	33 (55)	18 (30)	32 (27)	133 (44)	42 (70)	23 (38)	7 (12)	14 (12)	86 (29)	1.68^NS	1.87^NS	2.42*	2.93**	3.82^@
2.	Government hospitals	8 (13)	17 (28)	30 (50)	68 (57)	123 (41)	14 (23)	32 (53)	42 (70)	93 (78)	181 (60)	1.43^NS	2.79**	2.24*	3.47^@	4.65^@
3.	Homeopathic doctors	2 (5)	3 (5)	8 (13)	12 910)	26 (9)	3 (5)	3 (5)	8 (13)	12 (10)	26 (9)	–	–	–	–	–
4.	Anganwadi centres	12 (20)	31 (52)	33 (55)	65 (54)	141 (47)	20 (33)	43 (72)	47 (78)	103 (86)	213 (71)	1.61^NS	2.26*	2.67**	5.41^@	5.98^@
5.	Nativ practitioners	1 (2)	3 (5)	7 (12)	14 (12)	25 (8)	2 (3)	5 (8)	15 (25)	33 (28)	55 (18)	0.35^NS	0.67^NS	1.83^NS	3.10**	3.64^@
6.	Help from community health worker	16 (27)	34 (57)	30 (50)	68 (57)	148 (49)	23 (38)	43 (72)	41 (68)	100 (83)	207 (69)	1.29^NS	1.72^NS	2.00*	4.39^@	4.98^@

(Contd.)

Table 21 : (Contd.)

Sl. No.	Health Based coping Mechanisms adapted	Number of families: Peak Season LF	Peak MF	Peak SF	Peak LL	Peak OAF	Lean Season LF	Lean MF	Lean SF	Lean LL	Lean OAF	'Z' Value LF	'Z' MF	'Z' SF	'Z' LL	'Z' OAF
7.	Directly from medical stores	5 (8)	11 (18)	13 (22)	26 (22)	55 (18)	8 (13)	16 (27)	18 (30)	38 (32)	80 (27)	0.89 NS	1.18 NS	1.00 NS	1.74 NS	2.64**
8.	Adapting home	6 (10)	16 (27)	20 (33)	43 (36)	85 (28)	6 (10)	22 (37)	32 (53)	69 (58)	129 (43)	–	1.17 NS	2.21 NS	3.41@	3.84@
9.	Postponement of treatment	0	2 (3)	5 (8)	11 (9)	18 (6)	2 (3)	12 (20)	26 (43)	58 (48)	98 (33)	1.35 NS	2.92**	4.40@	6.69@	0.35@
10.	Postponment of minor operations	0	6 (10)	9 (15)	22 918)	37 (12)	0	8 (13)	18 (30)	42 935)	68 (23)	–	0.52 NS	1.97 NS	2.98**	3.55@
11.	Undergoing family planning operations at Government hospitals	2 (3)	3 (5)	3 (5)	7 (6)	15 (5)	2 (3)	3 (5)	5 (8)	8 (7)	18 (6)	–	–	0.67 NS	0.31 NS	0.54 NS
12.	No treatment was taken	0	6 (10)	15 (25)	31 (26)	52 (17)	1 (2)	13 (22)	26 (43)	53 (44)	93 (31)	1.10 NS	1.79 NS	2.08*	2.92**	4.01@

Figures within parenthesis indicate percentage.

NS = Not significant; * = Significant at 5% level; ** = Significant at 1% level; @ = Significant at 0.1% level.

Health Based Coping Mechanisms

1. Private clinics
2. Government hospitals
3. Homeopathic doctors
4. Anganwadi centres
5. Native practitioners
6. Help from comunity health worker
7. Directlyfrom medical stores
8. Adapting home remedies
9. Postponement of treatment
10. Postponement of minor operatons.
11. Undergoing family planning operations at Government hospitals.
12. No treatment was taken.

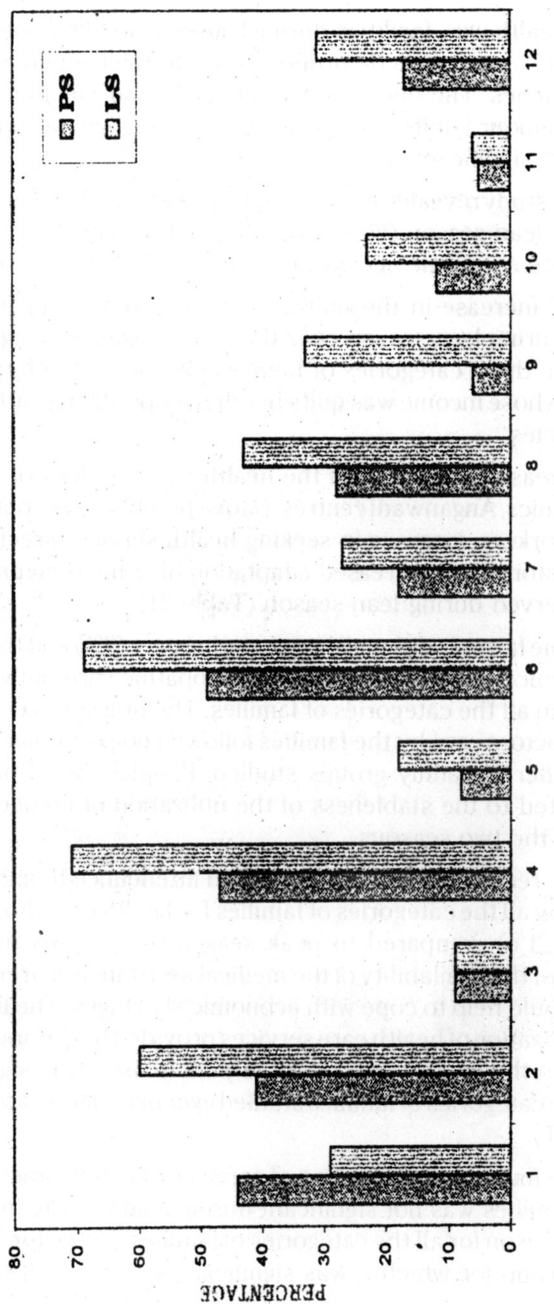

Fig. 14 : Distribution of Families According to Health Based Coping Mechanisms Adapted

private health care facilities during lean season (29%), over peak season (44%) was directly proportionate to the land holding size of the families. The decrease was significant for small farm and landless labour families. But for large and medium farm families it was not significant.

The study revealed increased utilization of government health clinics in lean season (60%) over the peak season (41%) due to inadequate economic access of the families in lean season.

The increase in the utilization of government health care service during lean season over the peak season was significant for all the three categories of families except for the large farm families whose income was quite better to cope atleast with health emergencies.

Increased utilization of the health care services of Homeopathic clinics, Anganwadi centres, Native practitioners community health workers, increase in seeking health service directly from medical stores and increased adaptation of home remedies were also observed during lean season (Table 21).

Some farmers did avail homeopathic care (9%) and there was no difference in the availment of homeopathic care between the seasons in all the categories of families. The utilization of homeopathic doctors care by the families followed no particular pattern in the different family groups studied. People's belief might be contributed to the stableness of the utilization of homeo clinics between the two seasons.

The results revealed an increased attendance to anganwadi centres by all the categories of families for health care during lean season (71%) compared to peak season (47%). This might be because of the availability of the medical assistance on free of cost which would help to cope with economic shortages. The increase in the utilization of health care services provided by the anganwadi centres in the lean season over the peak season was significant for all the categories of families studied except for large farm group (Table 21).

The increase in utilization of services of native practitioners by the families was not significant during lean season compared to peak season for all the categories of families except for landless labour group for which it was significant at 1 per cent level.

Increase in lean period over the peak was also observed in the practice of adapting home remedies such as giving pepper juice among the medium, small farm and landless labour families. Increase in the practice was not observed among the large farm group. The increase was significant at 1 per cent and 0.1 per cent level among small farm and landless labour groups. With regard to medium farm families increase in the adaptation of this practice was not significant. (Table 23).

The dry spell in the study regions also led the adaptation of hard options like postponement of treatment and postponement of minor operations. Large farm families even though were not reported of postponement of treatment during the peak season, they reported the same in lean season indicating the crises created by the dry season (Fig. 14). The increase in the practice of postponement of treatment during the lean season over the peak season was significant for the medium, small farm and landless labour groups (Table 21).

Large farm families did not adapt the hard option of postponement of minor operations. The increase in the adaptation of this health based coping mechanism by the medium farm and small farm families was not significant and only for the landless labour households the increase was significant at 1 per cent level (Table 21).

The families underwent family planning operations in both the seasons. The difference between the two seasons was not statistically significant for all the categories of families studied in the adaptation of this health based coping mechanism. A slight increase in the family planning operations during lean season over the peak season might be due to the availability of leisure time.

On the whole the increase in the practice of not taking treatment in the lean season was significant at 0.1 per cent level. Large farm families did not opt this hard health based coping mechanisms atleast in peak season, though not in lean season. In general, adaptation of the health based coping mechanism by the four groups was indirectly related to the ownership of the land in both seasons studied (Table 23).

To conclude, in the event of illness, households were faced with alternative choice between self-care and an array of providers, including government clinics, private doctors, chemists, homeo doctors, anganwadi services, traditional healers, home remedies and community health services. They did not mind to postpone treatment or to postpone minor operations or undergoing family planning operations for the sake of money or even not taking the treatment at all. Where these providers were known and available, the choice was to be a product of such factors as quality of care, price of treatment, distance, education of fatter the mother and last but not least was the income of the household, taking into consideration household budget constraints.

The coping mechanisms adapted for food security at household level are summarised into 3 options viz., "better options", "frugal options" and "hard options" and are presented in Table 22, From the table, it was clear that most of the better options were directly proportionate and the frugal and hard options were indirectly proportionate to the land owned.

Over the years of famine and drought the households developed some mechanisms to cope with difficult situations in that they adapt better options at the quest then go for frugal options and hard option which were adapted as a last resort in acute food shortages.

Information collected based on the coping mechanisms adapted can be used by planners and policy makers in preparing and implementing short term food intervention strategies such as targeting of food aid by shifting food to an area which is most affected by drought and opening seasonal markets. Food price stabilization can be achieved by analyzing existing price situation in various parts of the country as a medium - term food security strategy. Long term strategies such as improving infrastructure, intensifying the cropping pattern, and continuous monitoring & effective implementation of ongoing welfare programmes can lead to increased food availability.

Table 22 : Summary of coping mechanisms adapted for food security at household level by the families

Sl. No.	Coping mechanisms	Per cent of families				
		LF	*MF*	*SF*	*LL*	*OAF*
I. Better Options						
1.	Intercrop adjustents of cropped area	88	77	63	NA	76
2.	Use of Farm Yard manure	100	100	100	NA	100
3.	Use of chemical fertilizers	95	78	67	NA	80
4.	Use of Pesticides	60	33	27	NA	40
5.	Use of Weedicides	50	15	3	NA	23
6.	Use of seed treatment procedures	80	58	47	NA	62
7.	Use of hybrid/improved seeds	93	87	72	NA	84
8.	Use of canal water or tank water for irrigation	30	17	10	NA	19
9.	Use of well or borewell water for irrigation	33	13	0	NA	16
10.	Use of lift irrigation method	3	0	0	NA	1
11.	Seeking support from State Ahgricultural Department	–	30	37	NA	13
12.	Seeking support from State Veterinary Department	7	12	22	27	16
13.	Deepening of wells	3	2	0	NA	2
14.	Digging well or borewell	2	0	0	NA	1
15.	Increase in non-farm occupations during lean season	6	7	23	26	17
16.	Increase in working on small trades during lean season	4	6	8	3	5
17.	Participating in welfare programmes (PDS/ICDS/DWCRA/JRY/RDI/YIP)	83	97	100	100	96
18.	Opting to work for kind	0	23	37	42	29
19.	Increase in sending children to AWC	18	20	22	25	22

Contd.

Table 22 : (Contd.)

Sl. No.	Coping mechanisms	Per cent of families				
		LF	*MF*	*SF*	*LL*	*OAF*
20.	Increase in collecting forest produce for food and generation of income	12	22	68	78	52
21.	Increase in procuring unconventional foods	0	8	10	13	9
22.	Storing staples	73	57	42	28	46
23.	Storing tamarind and red chillies for one year	100	100	100	100	100
24.	Storing the major crops produced and selling during economic crisis	53	28	10	0	18
25.	Substitution of millets to rice and horsegram or cowpea to redgram	10	28	77	88	58
26.	Curtailment in the use of intoxicants, cigarettes and pan	35	43	48	48	45
27.	Decrease in seeking health services from private clinics	13	17	18	15	16
28.	Increase in seeking health services from					
	PHC	10	25	20	21	19
	AWC	13	20	23	32	24
	CHS	12	15	18	27	20
29.	Undergoing family planning operations at Government hospitals	0	0	3	1	1
II.	**Frugal Options**					
1.	Foraging in common property	22	17	18	15	17
2.	Remittances from parents and relatives	7	32	43	50	36
3.	Cooking only once in a day	33	48	62	72	57
4.	Postponement of functions other than marriages	5	13	15	17	13

Contd.

Table 22 : (Contd.)

Sl. No.	*Coping mechanisms*	*Per cent of families*				
		LF	*MF*	*SF*	*LL*	*OAF*
5.	Postponement or avoiding travel or travelling by walk	5	18	25	32	22
6.	Curtailment of recreation like cinema	5	20	25	25	20
7.	Increase in seeking health services from native practitioners	2	3	13	16	10
8.	Increase in taking home remedies	0	10	20	22	15
III.	Hard Options					
1.	Shrinking of net sown area	83	98	100	NA	94
2.	Reduction in livestock owned due to selling, gifting and abandoning	16	13	12	6	11
3a.	Liquidation of farm assets	7	15	25	NA	14
b.	Liquidation of non-farm assets	3	7	10	10	8
4.	Postponement of acquisition of all common durables	58	93	95	100	89
5.	Curtailment in the expenditure on all food & non-food items	100	100	100	100	100
6.	Increase in institutional or private borrowing	17	22	20	20	20
7.	Accepting to work for low wages almost half that of peak season wages	10	22	43	47	34
8.	Employing children for borrowing money	–	–	5	12	6
9.	Taking loans (grains)	–	–	5	8	6
10.	Begging (grain/money)	–	–	2	2	1
11.	Decrease in procuring foods grown or produced in own farms	50	65	83	NA	66

Contd.

Table 22 : (Contd.)

Sl. No.	*Coping mechanisms*	*Per cent of families*				
		LF	*MF*	*SF*	*LL*	*OAF*
12.	Decrease in procuring foods through PDS	5	50	67	77	55
13.	Procuring cheaper quality foods	13	33	43	44	36
14.	Decrease in purchasing foods by paying cash	10	27	50	53	38
15.	Increase in purchasing foods on loan	0	0	5	8	4
16.	Eating the grain kept for seed purpose	3	17	20	NA	13
17.	Curtailment in number of meals from 3 to 2 in a day	10	93	95	98	79
18.	Reducing meal size	7	93	95	100	79
19.	Curtailment in consumption of protective foods	7	95	97	98	79
20.	Curtailment in consumption of coffee and tea or diluting the milk	15	33	72	79	56
21.	Diluting the milk or giving coffee or tea instead of milk to the children	8	22	62	72	47
22.	Changing meal pattern with chutnies and other available foods in place of vegetable curries and dhal	2	22	50	59	38
23.	Use of more puffed rice	0	27	32	35	26
24.	Curtailing work and activities to supress hunger	0	3	8	11	7
25.	Forceful starvation	0	5	7	8	5
26.	Sending daughter-in-law alongwith children to parents house or children to grand parents house	3	12	22	22	16

Contd.

Table 22 : (Contd.)

Sl. No.	*Coping mechanisms*	*Per cent of families*				
		LF	*MF*	*SF*	*LL*	*OAF*
27.	Avoiding guests, relatives, friends, gifts and beggers	7	17	53	78	47
28.	Maintaining the secrecy of resources in the forest	0	2	12	23	12
29.	Seeking health services directly from medical shops	5	8	8	10	8
30.	Postponement of treatment	3	17	35	39	27
31.	Postponement of minor operations	0	3	15	17	10
32.	Not taking the treatment	2	12	18	18	14

NA = Not applicable

Food & Nutrient Intake and Nutritional Status of Women and Preschool, Children

Food & Nutrient Intake of Women and Preschool Children

Food Intake

Mean food intake of women and preschool children is given in Table 23 and 24 respectively. Food adequacy of women and preschool children is given in Table 25, and Fig. 15.

Cereals and Millets

It was noted that during lean season, the mean consumption cereals by the women decreased and the consumption of millets increased significantly for all the categories of families studied. Similarly, there was an increase in millet consumption and decrease in cereal consumption by the preschool children in lean season over the peak season tough it was not found to be significant.

From the observations it could be inferred that even though rice was supplied on substituted price through PDS during lean season, the farming community developed the habit of storing the milestone plenty, for use in economic shortage that would occur in dry season as a preventive coping mechanism to withstand the economic burden.

Table 23 : Mean food intake of women (g/day)

(n=18 for LF, MF & SF, n=35 for LL, n=90 for OAF)

Sl. No.	Food Groups	Peak Season LF	Peak Season MF	Peak Season SF	Peak Season LL	Peak Season OAF	Lean Season LF	Lean Season MF	Lean Season SF	Lean Season LL	Lean Season OAF	't' Value LF	't' Value MF	't' Value SF	't' Value LL	't' Value OAF
1.	Cereals	412.50	484.50	424.60	437.80	439.41	326.40	296.20	271.50	253.40	280.20	2.72@	5.59@	5.50@	9.12@	11.52@
2.	Millets	28.20	64.30	75.00	92.20	70.40	82.90	108.20	128.90	155.80	126.30	3.23*	2.28*	2.50*	3.78**	5.52@
3.	Pulses	51.50	38.10	43.00	46.80	45.20	36.90	18.60	21.20	26.10	25.80	1.78^{NS}	3.03**	2.99**	4.03@	5.87@
4.	GLVs	3.40	4.10	5.30	7.60	5.60	13.30	14.10	17.70	17.70	16.09	2.50*	2.19*	2.30*	2.26*	4.39@
5.	Roots & Tubers	11.20	10.60	9.18	11.70	10.86	49.10	45.00	47.80	34.10	42.02	2.36*	2.18*	2.18*	2.20*	4.49@
6.	Other vegetables	70.4	51.50	46.40	42.70	50.70	34.90	20.70	21.40	16.60	22.05	2.14*	2.33*	2.26*	3.25**	4.94@
7.	Fruits	9.80	7.40	8.90	7.60	8.30	7.30	5.00	6.40	5.30	5.90	0.40^{NS}	0.50^{NS}	0.43^{NS}	0.65^{NS}	1.01^{NS}
8.	Milk	72.00	30.30	42.63	36.80	43.70	33.70	11.60	16.80	18.10	19.70	3.19**	2.74**	2.59**	3.18**	5.47@
9.	Meat/fish/ chicken/eggs	12.60	2.00	2.00	9.30	7.10	8.40	0.00	0.00	2.50	2.70	0.64^{NS}	1.00^{NS}	1.30^{NS}	1.66^{NS}	1.97^{NS}
10.	Sugar & Jaggery	16.70	13.50	14.90	14.90	15.00	6.40	3.70	4.40	4.50	4.70	5.86@	6.73@	6.96@	9.28@	14.49@
11.	Fats & Oils	9.60	7.46	6.60	6.80	7.50	5.30	3.70	2.10	2.60	3.30	3.60@	3.37**	4.36@	7.08@	8.81@
12.	Nuts & Oilseeds	19.50	27.70	22.0	19.30	21.60	13.80	21.90	18.20	16.70	17.50	1.05^{NS}	1.00^{NS}	0.72^{NS}	0.69^{NS}	1.69^{NS}

NS : Not significant, * Significant at 5% level, ** Significant at 1% level, @ Significant at 0.1% level

Table 24 : Mean food intake of Pre-school Children (g/day)

(n=18 for LF, MF & SF, n=36 for LL, n=90 for OAF)

Sl. No.	Food Groups	Peak Season LF	MF	SF	LL	OAF	Lean Season LF	MF	SF	LL	OAF	't' Value LF	MF	SF	LL	OAF
1.	Cereals	249.00	221.00	227.30	256.60	242.10	238.20	198.60	213.30	237.50	225.00	0.37^{NS}	0.84^{NS}	0.49^{NS}	1.03^{NS}	1.39^{NS}
2.	Millets	12.20	15.80	35.60	57.20	35.60	16.50	26.70	50.40	63.60	44.20	1.07^{NS}	1.90^{NS}	1.55^{NS}	0.81^{NS}	1.77^{NS}
3.	Pulses	20.30	19.90	19.40	21.70	20.60	14.40	8.10	7.10	10.20	10.00	1.58^{NS}	3.59**	3.79$^{@}$	4.66$^{@}$	6.86$^{@}$
4.	GLVs	1.10	1.80	2.30	2.50	2.10	7.10	4.90	7.11	8.31	7.15	2.39*	2.19*	2.13*	2.14*	3.80$^{@}$
5.	Roots & Tubers	4.90		5.70	7.00	6.00	22.30	20.50	26.30	25.40	24.00	2.13*	2.19*	2.13*	2.14*	3.80$^{@}$
6.	Other vegetables	33.00	.50	23.80	25.10	26.70	19.10	12.00	12.50	14.20	14.40	2.21*	2.28*	2.15*	2.42*	44.9$^{@}$
7.	Fruits	15.70	10.50	17.80	14.60	14.60	9.20	6.80	14.00	9.20	9.70	0.70^{NS}	0.53^{NS}	0.34^{NS}	0.78^{NS}	1.18^{NS}
8.	Milk	157.40	123.80	133.60	117.40	129.90	79.10	48.00	52.40	45.80	54.21	5.10$^{@}$	5.77^{NS}	5.30^{NS}	7.36^{NS}	11.44^{NS}
9.	Meat/fish/ chicken/eggs	8.50	1.00	1.00	3.50	3.50	2.60	0.00	0.00	0.00	0.51	1.61^{NS}	1.00^{NS}	1.00^{NS}	1.91^{NS}	2.71**
10.	Sugar & Jaggery	21.20	18.20	17.60	14.10	17.00	11.20	8.40	6.70	6.70	7.60	3.87$^{@}$	4.51$^{@}$	4.75$^{@}$	4.34$^{@}$	8.33$^{@}$
11.	Fats & Oils	5.30	4.00	4.10	4.40	4.40	2.60	1.60	1.80	2.00	2.00	3.14**	3.46$^{@}$	3.45**	4.21$^{@}$	7.08$^{@}$
12.	Nuts & Oilseeds	12.30	17.20	14.80	10.90	13.20	8.90	14.70	11.40	9.00	10.60	1.13^{NS}	0.58^{NS}	0.99^{NS}	0.97^{NS}	1.76^{NS}

NS : Not significant, * Significant at 5% level, ** Significant at 1% level, @ Significant at 0.1% level

Table 25 : Food Adequacy* of Women and Pre-school Children

Food Groups	Peak season					Lean season				
	LF	*MF*	*SF*	*LL*	*OAF*	*LF*	*MF*	*SF*	*LL*	*OAF*
1. Cereals										
Women	130	115	123	128	12	77	68	64	60	67
PSC	125	104	99	100	107	112	96	87	89	96
2. Millets										
Women	7	15	18	22	16	20	25	30	37	28
PSC	7	9	20	33	17	9	15	29	36	22
3. Cereals+ Millets										
Women	137	130	141	150	140	97	93	94	97	95
PSC	132	113	119	133	124	121	111	116	125	118
4. Pulses										
Women	80	61	67	73	70	58	29	33	39	40
PSC	41	40	39	43	41	29	16	14	21	20
5. GLVs										
Women	3	3	4	4	4	10	15	17	16	15
PSC	2	3	5	4	4	9	10	12	11	11
6. Roots & Tubers										
Women	15	14	17	16	16	65	60	53	45	56
PSC	12	14	14	17	14	57	51	59	64	58
7. Other Vegetables										
Women	85	55	56	51	62	40	25	26	23	29
PSC	83	66	59	63	68	48	29	31	36	36
8. Fruits										
Women	33	25	30	25	28	24	17	21	18	20
PSC	18	14	18	18	17	31	21	28	29	27
9. Milk										
Women	50	21	23	26	30	23	8	10	10	13
PSC	66	52	56	49	56	33	20	22	19	24

Contd....

Table 25 : (Contd.)

Food Groups	Peak season					Lean season				
	LF	MF	SF	LL	OAF	LF	MF	SF	LL	OAF
10. Meat/fish/ chicken/ eggs										
Women	9	4	4	6	6	5	–	–	2	2
PSC	5	2	2	3	3	2	–	–	–	1
11. Sugar & Jaggery										
Women	38	31	34	34	34	15	8	10	10	11
PSC	61	52	50	41	51	32	18	20	19	22
12. Fats & Oils										
Women	22	17	15	15	17	12	8	5	6	8
PSC	23	17		19	19	12	5	8	7	8
13. Nuts & Oilseeds										
Women	40	69	55	48	53	35	55	45	42	44
PSC	–	–	–	–	–	–	–	–	–	–

*Gopalan *et al.* (1991)
PSC = Pre-school children

It is worthwhile to bring the fact here that as reported by the families under "food consumption based mechanisms", the men and women were mostly following two meal pattern in lean season and no change was found in the number of meals of children in all the categories of families studied. The results reported by Kamany (1978) in Zaire of Bas-Zaire region revealed that when cassava, the staple of the village was insufficient, young children received them only after the needs of man in the households. This variations in intra family distribution of the main staple between the two seasons observed showed a critical condition faced and the resultant alternative hard coping mechanism followed by the families during the times of dry spells in these drought prone regions to meet the shortages of the food needs.

Pulses

It was observed that the mean intake of pulse by both the women and preschool children was significantly lower in lean

Food Groups

1. Cereals
2. Millets
3. Cereals+millets
4. Pulses
5. GLVs
6. Roots & Tubers
7. Other Vegetables
8. Fruits
9. Milk
10. Meat/fish/chicken/eggs
11. Sugar & Jaggery
12. Fats & Oils
13. Nuts & Oilseeds

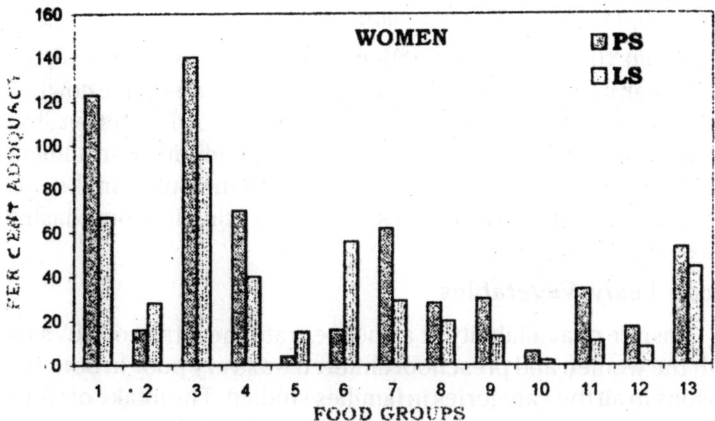

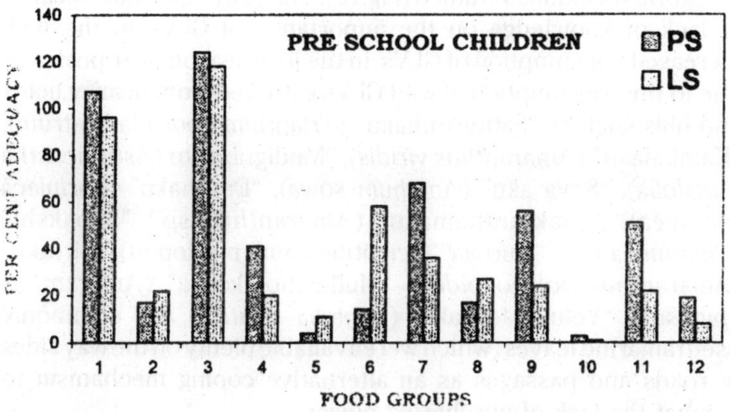

Fig. 15: Food Adequacy of Women and Pre-School Children

season compared to peak season in all the categories of families, except for large farm families for which the intake showed no significant decrease between the seasons in both women and preschool children (Table 23 and 24).

From the food consumption records it was observed the during lean season the families replaced pepper dhals like cowpea and horsegram to redgram reflecting the stress of destitution shift in the usage of costly pulses as food expenditure curtailment adaptation to the possible extent. Even then the pulse intake was decreased significantly in lean season indicating low purchasing power of the families.

Green Leafy Vegetables

Inspite of availability at a cheaper rate the intake of GLVs by both the women and preschool children was very poor in both the seasons in all the categories in families studied. The intake of GLVs by both the women and preschool children during lean season was significant higher compared to peak season for all the groups (Table 23 and 24)

The intake of GLVs by both women and preschool children was much below the RDA of ICMR in both seasons in all the categories of families studied (Fig.15). This may be mainly because of lack of knowledge on the importance of GLVs in the diet. Increased consumption of GLVs in the lean season over peak was due to the consumption of wild GLVs gathered from nearby fields and hills such as "Sathwanthaku" (*Trianthima portula castrum*), "Kambalaku" (*Amaranthus viridis*), "Mudigubbaku (*Asteracantha longifolia*), "Soya aku" (*Anethum sowa*), "Donthaku" (*Porlulaca oleracea*), "Chakranthamaku" (*Amaranthus sp.*) "Sabakshi" (*Pimpinella sp.*). "Guruga" (Scientific name not found), "Sirraku" (*Amaranthus polygonoides*), "Mulla thotakoora" (*Amaranthus spinosus*), "Yeluka Jeevaku" (*Centella asiatica*) and commonly used tamarind leaves (which were available plenty on the way sides of roads and passages as an alternative coping mechanism to combat the lack of purchasing power.

It is worthwhile to mention here that during the investigation period specially in the month of April and May it was observed that most of the families used that dhal prepared with tamarind leaves along with millet preparation.

Roots & Tubers

The consumption of roots & tubers was very poor in both seasons in all groups of women and preschool children. The intake of roots & tubers by both women and preschool children increased significantly (5% level) during lean season over the peak season among all the four categories of families (Table 25 and 26). This was mainly because of the consumption of wild roots & tubers. The tuber used was the lower portion of the flowering agave (Agave Linn) stalk of plant. Similar results were also reported by Swaminathan (1967). In one of the study conducted at Ananthapur.

Other Vegetables

A significant decrease was observed in the mean intake of other vegetables in all the categories of women and preschool children in lean season compared to peak season (Table 23 and 24). Consumption of vegetables other than brinjal and gourds was very low.

Fruits

A significant decrease was not found in the consumption of fruits by both the women and preschool children in the lean season over peak season among all the categories of families studied.

Infact, the average consumption of the fruits by the preschool children was higher than the women in both the seasons among all the categories of farming groups. This was because of the children's habit to go round, collect and consume the wild fruits such as palm berries, country beer and goose berries etc.

Women and preschool children in all the categories of families in both seasons did not include fruits at all in their diet during the days of deity survey (Fig.15). In other words it could be said that fruits were virtually absent in their diets.

Milk

The intake of milk was significantly lower during lean season compared to peak season in both women and preschool children (Table 23 & 24).

The milk purchased for 50 Paise or Rs. 1.00, specially during lean season was mostly given to children and otherwise used for tea. Use of curds in the meal was very rare. The lower milk intake by low income groups was reported by Satyanarayana (1972) and

Pushpamma *et al.* (1981). NNMB (1990-92) investigated the food intake and nutrient adequacy of rural population in Andhra Pradesh and found that the intake of milk was very poor in all the age groups.

Among the women and preschool children of large farm groups also the intake of milk was significantly lower in lean season over peak period. Even the families who were producing the milk were not consuming the required amounts of milk particularly in lean period for want of money to meet the staple shortages. Children were given only tea in place of milk and not given any other milk products specially in lean spells.

Fleshy Foods & Eggs

Consumption of fleshy foods by both the women and preschool children was low in both the seasons among all the farming communities studied. Very few families occasionally consumed meat & eggs and the diet was almost lacking in meat, fish & eggs (Fig. 15).

Sugar & Jaggery

The consumption of sugar & jaggery was significantly lower at 0.1% level in the season, over peak season in both women and preschool children of all the categories of families.

Fats & Oils

The mean intake of fats & oils was significantly lower for all the categories of women and preschool children studied in lean season compared to peak season (Table 23 & 24).

Nuts & Oilseeds

Significant difference was not observed in the mean consumption of nuts & oilseeds among different categories of women and preschool children between the seasons. This was mainly due to the frequent consumption of groundnut as Ananthapur is predominantly the groundnut cultivating area.

Lowered consumption of protective foods like pulses, milk, GLVs, egg &other flesh foods by the rural families was also reported in studies conducted by Asthrukar (1977) in Parbhani, Deva Das (1983) in Andhra Pradesh, Bhat (1985) in Gangwa village, Hissar district, Rama Devi (1986) and Shailaja (1986) in Andhra Pradesh, Nagamalleswari (1989) in Rangareddy district, Andhra Pradesh and the studied carried out by NIN (1987) in 5 states of India (Gujarath, Andhra Pradesh, Orissa, Tamilnadu and Karnataka).

Studies carried out by Swaminathan (1969) in Bihar, Krishnamachari (1974) in Maharastra and the studies carried out by NIN (1987) in 5 states of India namely Gujarath, Andhra Pradesh, Orissa, Tamilnadu and Karnataka also revealed lowered consumption of cereals, increased consumption of millets, GLVs and roots & tubers, specially of wild GLVs and roots & tubers such as 'Siriaku' 'Gadhakaku' (Botanical names not available) and 'agave' (*Agave Linn*) etc., and decreased consumption of protective foods (pulses, milk egg & other fleshy foods, fats & oils and sugar & jagger) by the rural families during drought periods compared to non-drought periods. The results of the present study are also comparable with the above results.

The mean intake of all foods except millets, GLVs and roots & tubers were lower during lean season over the peak season in all the categories of families. Significant change was observed between the seasons in the consumption of all the foods except in the fruits and nuts & oil seeds in both women and preschool children of four categories of families. This was because fruits were virtually absent in their diets and groundnuts is the predominant crop grown in the area.

In conclusion, it could be reported that only the intake of cereals & millets was meeting the recommended dietary allowance and the intake of all other foods was much below the requirements in both the seasons for women and preschool children of all categories of families studied (Table 25).

Comparison of per cent adequacy in the intake of total staples and all other cereals foods by both women and preschool children in both seasons and among all the categories of farming groups studied revealed the fact that the families with past experience made a hard option of coping with dry spells of food shortages and were maintaining at least the consumption level of staple at the cost of all other non cereals consumables.

The comparison of consumption of commodities by the medium farm, small farm and landless labour families in both peak and lean seasons showed that there was no marked difference in their consumption habits i.e. either in quantities or number of items consumed (Table 23 & 24). As such it was clear that small area of land could not bring any considerable changes in consumption level and composition of goods in these three categories of families.

However, difference between large farmer families over other three categories of families in both peak and lean season was marked in that these large farm families not only consumed more quantities under essential items and some new items like snack and breakfast preparations were added their list of foods.

Nutrient Intake of Women and Preschool Children

The mean nutrient intake of women and preschool children is presented in Table 26, and 27 and the per cent nutrient adequacy is given in Table 28 and Fig. 16.

Energy

The mean calorie intake of women and preschool children during lean season, over peak did not decrease significantly for all the categories of families.

Bidinger (1990) reported of lowered energy intake by the rural families in Dokur, a Telangana village of Andhra Pradesh. A study conducted by Thimmayamma (1982) in 176 urban and 171 rural households in Hyderabad revealed that in rural preschool children the calorie adequacy was 83 per cent irrespective of income. The results of the present study were lower than these values (peak season - 80% and lean present - 71%).

Though the consumption of cereals was slightly more than the RDA, their diets were deficient in energy, because they consumed negligible amounts of fat which is a rich source of energy. The reduction in calorie adequacy followed no particular pattern among the various groups studied in both women and preschool children. Braun *et al.* (1992) study in various developing countries such as Brazil, Gautemala, Gambira, Kenya, Rwanda, Sri Lanka, Bangladesh, India and Phillippines also revealed that the income had no effect no calorie adequacy.

It was noted that inspite of ail being supplied through fair price shops consumption of the same was not adequate which was due to high cost. Preschool children were mostly fed with "rasam" or butter milk along with mashed rice without any vegetables or dhals, because of the fear of digestion problem.

Protein

The mean intake of protein by both women and preschool children was significantly lower in lean season compared to peak

Table 26 : Mean Nutrient Intake of Women (per day)

(n=18 for LF, MF & SF, n=36 for LL, n=90 for OAF)

Nutrients	Peak Season					Lean Season					't' Value				
	LF	MF	SF	LL	OAF	LF	MF	SF	LL	OAF	LF	MF	SF	LL	OAF
Calorie (K.cals)	2147.80	1967.70	2066.60	2205.60	2118.70	2105.17	1898.30	2048.72	2079.69	2042.32	0.49^{NS}	1.08^{NS}	0.20^{NS}	2.01^{NS}	1.95^{NS}
Protein (g)	58.90	49.00	52.10	54.40	53.70	35.10	26.10	30.80	28.46	29.80	$9.47^{@}$	$8.95^{@}$	$8.89^{@}$	$11.84^{@}$	$18.45^{@}$
Fats(g)	29.20	21.20	20.40	19.90	22.10	22.20	14.30	13.90	15.10	16.10	2.56*	2.25*	2.21*	$3.70^{@}$	$4.91^{@}$
Calcium (mg)	389.30	248.20	296.70	304.70	308.70	296.70	132.67	172.70	192.30	197.30	3.73**	$5.03^{@}$	$6.49^{@}$	$4.95^{@}$	$7.97^{@}$
Iron (mg)	20.10	13.70	17.10	16.00	16.60	16.60	11.60	13.80	13.60	13.80	1.68^{NS}	1.67^{NS}	2.02^{NS}	1.80^{NS}	3.31**
Thiamine (mg)	1.32	1.07	1.17	1.39	1.27	1.64	1.31	1.44	1.61	1.52	2.04^{NS}	1.45^{NS}	1.73^{NS}	1.82^{NS}	3.40**
Riboflavin (mg)	0.73	0.46	0.61	0.66	0.63	1.12	0.76	0.97	0.89	0.93	2.14*	2.43*	2.24*	2.28*	$4.41^{@}$
B-crotene (ug)	310.20	244.00	266.30	295.95	282.50	293.00	224.40	243.10	278.00	263.31	0.27^{NS}	0.48^{NS}	0.45^{NS}	0.41^{NS}	0.76^{NS}
Ascorbic acid (mg)	20.50	12.07	10.20	13.80	14.08	28.80	17.52	15.23	18.20	19.60	1.88^{NS}	2.54*	2.38*	2.44*	$3.91^{@}$

NS : Not significant, * Significant at 5% level, ** Significant at 1% level, @ Significant at 0.1% level

Table 27 : Mean Nutrient Intake of pre-school children (per day)

(n=18 for LF, MF & SF, n=36 for LL, n=90 for OAF)

Nutrients	*Peak Season*					*Lean Season*					*'t' Value*				
	LF	*MF*	*SF*	*LL*	*OAF*	*LF*	*MF*	*SF*	*LL*	*OAF*	*LF*	*MF*	*SF*	*LL*	*OAF*
Calorie (K.cals)	1069.20	887.20	961.70	1028.56	995.40	1007.50	805.70	885.60	962.80	924.90	0.73^{NS}	1.05^{NS}	1.02^{NS}	1.15^{NS}	1.92^{NS}
Protein (g)	31.20	23.20	29.50	26.50	26.60	17.40	12.80	15.50	15.00	15.10	3.76**	5.09$^{@}$	4.70$^{@}$	6.02$^{@}$	9.29$^{@}$
Fats(g)	15.80	13.00	12.40	13.10	13.50	10.20	7.50	7.20	9.00	8.60	2.41*	2.47*	2.40*	2.63*	4.93$^{@}$
Calcium (mg)	232.10	167.70	121.50	201.10	194.90	130.70	98.10	106.10	131.60	119.60	6.09$^{@}$	4.38$^{@}$	3.94**	4.71$^{@}$	8.77$^{@}$
Iron (mg)	11.90	9.30	0.30	7.40	8.60	6.50	5.10	4.40	4.50	5.00	5.44$^{@}$	3.35**	2.70*	3.42**	6.71$^{@}$
Thiamine (mg)	1.05	0.46	0.71	0.85	0.78	0.92	0.61	0.60	0.72	0.71	0.74^{NS}	1.55^{NS}	0.95^{NS}	1.89^{NS}	1.21^{NS}
Riboflavin (mg)	0.39	0.32	0.35	0.30	0.33	0.42	0.38	0.40	0.41	0.40	0.25^{NS}	0.61^{NS}	0.38^{NS}	1.75^{NS}	1.56^{NS}
B-crotene (ug)	186.11	149.20	182.90	169.00	165.20	175.30	138.50	148.80	157.90	155.70	0.44^{NS}	0.55^{NS}	0.21^{NS}	0.87^{NS}	1.05^{NS}
Ascorbic acid (mg)	11.59	7.22	8.58	8.50	8.70	13.19	10.30	11.44	11.44	11.50	0.70^{NS}	2.73*	2.44*	2.49*	3.73$^{@}$

NS : Not significant, * Significant at 5% level, ** Significant at 1% level, @ Significant at 0.1% level

Table 28 : Nutrient Adequacy* of Women and Pre-school Children

(n=18 for LF, MF & SF; n=36 for LL and N=90 for OAF)

Nutrients	Peak season					Lean season				
	LF	*MF*	*SF*	*LL*	*OAF*	*LF*	*MF*	*SF*	*LL*	*OAF*
1. Calorie										
Women	105	86	91	98	95	100	83	87	93	91
PSC	83	71	86	79	80	75	65	69	76	71
2. Protein										
Women	107	96	100	103	102	97	9	90	87	88
PSC	110	81	89	92	93	84	70	78	74	77
3. Fat										
Women	72	57	54	53	59	50	35	34	37	39
PSC	53	42	40	43	45	37	30	29	30	32
4. Calcium										
Women	49	31	37	38	39	38	16	22	2	25
PSC	58	42	43	50	48	33	25	27	32	29
5. Iron										
Women	61	42	52	48	51	51	35	42	41	42
PSC	70	58	45	49	56	41	32	27	27	32
6. Thiamine										
Women	106	86	94	112	100	134	106	116	130	122
PSC	123	91	98	96	102	140	82	95	109	107
7. Riboflavin										
Women	46	38	42	45	43	69	65	67	68	67
PSC	49	31	41	45	42	66	41	56	50	53
8. β-carotene										
Women	23	14	24	21	21	21	11	14	18	16
PSC	17	7	8	12	11	12	8	10	11	10
9. Ascorbic acid										
Women	49	33	29	36	37	63	43	39	44	47
PSC	30	19	19	21	22	30	26	29	20	30

*Gopalan *et al.* (1991)

PSC = Pre-school children

Nutrients

1. Calorie
2. Protein
3. Fat
4. Calcium
5. Iron
6. Thiamine
7. Riboflavin
8. β-carotene
9. Ascorbic acid

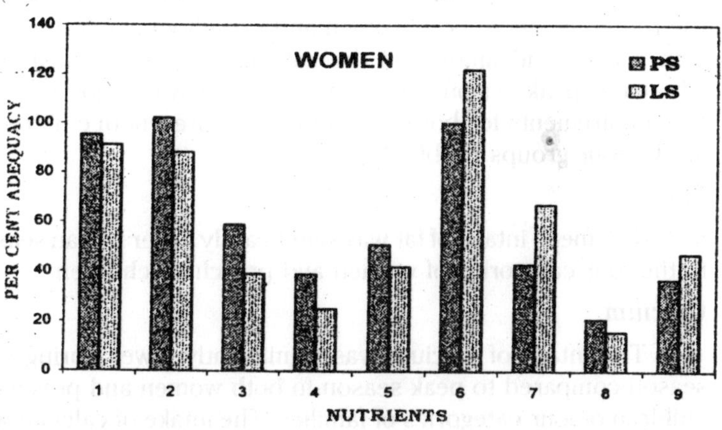

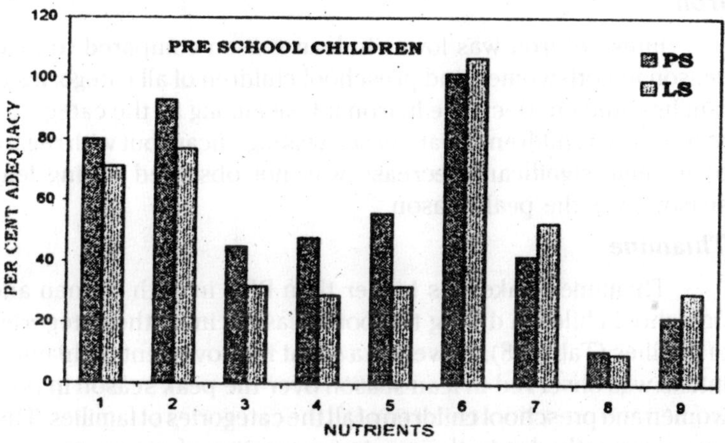

Fig. 16: Nutrrient Adequacy of Women and Pre-School Children

season. This trend was observed in all four groups (Table 28 & 29).

The per cent adequacy in the intake of protein was far below the requirements in both women and preschool children during lean season and among all the categories of families studied whereas in peak season the per cent adequacy was almost meeting the requirements for both the women and preschool children in all the four groups (Table 28).

Fat

The mean intake of fat was significantly lower in lean season in the four categories of women and preschool children.

Calcium

The intake of calcium was significantly lower during lean season compared to peak season in both women and preschool children of four categories of families. The intake of calcium was inadequate mainly due to poor consumption of protective foods such as milk, pulses, fleshy foods and fruits.

Iron

Intake of iron was lower in lean season compared to peak season in both women and preschool children of all categories of families studied. Decrease in iron intake among all the categories of preschool children in lean season was significant but with regard to women, significant decrease was not observed during lean season over the peak season.

Thiamine

Thiamine intake was higher than RDA in both women and preschool children during the both seasons in all the categories of families (Table 28). However, a slight improvement in thiamine intake was observed in lean season over the peak season in both women and preschool children of all the categories of families. This was apparently due to the greater proportion of coarse grains in their diets in lean season. However, the increase was not significant.

Riboflavin

Riboflavin was lacking in all diets particularly among pre-school children. This might be due to poor consumption of milk which is the rich source of riboflavin. NNMB (1990-92) reports revealed that the intake of riboflavin was inadequate in the sample surveyed in the state of kerala, Karnataka and Andhra Pradesh.

In women the increase in riboflavin intake was significant in lean season compared to peak season. In preschool children also increase in the riboflavin intake was observed during lean season but it showed no marked significance (Table 26 & 27). Intake of riboflavin was better in lean season than in peak season, due to increased consumption of coarse grains.

β-carotene

B-carotene was a limiting nutrient in both women and preschool children across of farm-size groups and in both seasons and there was little statistical evidence of variations between the seasons (Table 26, 27 & 28).

Pushpamma *et al.* (1981) also reported inadequate intake of vitamin A among rural population in Andhra Pradesh. NNMB (1990-92) reported that in none of the states studies (Kerala, Karnataka and Andhra Pradesh), the intake of vitamin A was adequate.

Ascorbic Acid

Respondents from all categories of farm size in both season showed major deficiencies in ascorbic acid intake. Pushpamma *et al.* (1981) also made similar observations of inadequate intake of vitamin C among rural population in three regions (Telangana, Rayalaseema and Coastal) of Andhra Pradesh.

Increased consumption of chutneys made from cucumber, tamarind and chillies in lean season led to significantly improved ascorbic acid intake by both women and preschool children of all the farming groups studied, except in large farm group, whose intake showed slight increase though not significant. But it was not adequate to alleviate the extreme dietary inadequacies (Table 26 & 27).

Studies carried out by Bhat (1985) preschool children of Gangwa village, Hissar district, Ramadevi (1986) and Sailaja (1986) studies in Andhra Pradesh, NIN (1987) study in Gujarath, Andhra Pradesh, Orissa, Tamilnadu, and Karanataka and Nagamalleswari (1989) study in Rangareddy district, Andhra Pradesh also reported of lowered consumption of nutrients such as proteins, B-complex vitamins, ascorbic acid, vitamin A, iron, Calcium by the rural families, ascorbic acid, vitamin A, iron, calcium by the rural families because of the lowered consumption of milk, pulses, GLVs and other protective foods. The results of the present study are comparable with the above results.

Swaminathan's (1987) study in Gujarath, Andhra Pradesh, Orissa, Tamilnadu and Karanataka states of India also revealed lowered consumption of energy, protein, fat and calcium during drought periods compared to non-drought periods. The present study also revealed lowered intake of the above mentioned nutrients in lean season compared to peak season.

The intake of thiamine, ascorbic acid and riboflavin increased during lean season over the "peak" mainly due to the increased consumption of millets, chutneys and other preparations made out of tamarind and chillies. These results are comparable with the results of Thomas Walker (1990) study in semi Arid Tropics.

On the whole, the nutrient adequacy showed that except calorie, protein and thiamine all the other nutrients, i.e. fat, calcium, iron, riboflavin, b-carotene and ascorbic acid were deficient in both women and preschool children in both seasons across all farm size groups mainly due to poor consumption of protective foods. In preschool children even the calorie and protein intake was below the requirement. Protein, fat and calcium showed significant difference across the seasons showing a decline in lean season among women and preschool children.

Nutritional Status of Women and Preschool Children

Anthropometric Measurements

Measurements of weight, height and arm circumference are commonly recognized as important indices of nutritional status i.e. of protein-energy malnutrition. Height is primarily a reflection of cumulative or past nutritional status, whereas the other measurement refers more to current or transitory nutritional status (Seoane and Lathaur, 1971).

Mean values of weight and height of women and mean values of weight, height and mid arm circumference of preschool children are presented in Table 29,

Significant difference in the mean anthropometric measurements was not found between the "peak" and "lean" seasons in both women and preschool children of the four categories of families.

The difference in the mean values of anthropometric measurements followed no particular pattern among the four groups studied in both the seasons.

Table 29 : Mean Anthropometric Measurements of Women and pre-school children

(n=18 for LF, MF & SF, n=36 for LL, n=90 for OAF)

Sl. No. Anthropometric measurements	Peak Season					Lean Season					't' Value				
	LF	MF	SF	LL	OAF	LF	MF	SF	LL	OAF	LF	MF	SF	LL	OAF
I. Women															
a) Weight(kg.)	44.86	46.50	42.94	42.72	43.95	44.75	46.44	42.78	42.63	43.85	0.02^{NS}	0.01^{NS}	0.03^{NS}	0.02^{NS}	0.02^{NS}
b) Height(cm)	148.71	151.72	146.50	145.18	147.46	148.76	151.79	146.57	145.21	147.51	0.01^{NS}	0.02^{NS}	0.01^{NS}	0.04^{NS}	0.07^{NS}
II. Pre-school Children															
a) Weight(kg)															
1–3 years	10.04	9.58	10.25	8.10	9.22	9.88	9.54	10.06	8.03	9.12	0.29^{NS}	0.05^{NS}	0.23^{NS}	0.17^{NS}	0.30^{NS}
3–5 years	13.08	12.25	12.85	11.81	12.36	12.92	12.00	12.80	11.69	12.22	0.24^{NS}	0.30^{NS}	0.07^{NS}	0.23^{NS}	0.36^{NS}
b) Height(cm)															
1–3 years	75.03	74.39	77.33	74.41	75.00	75.23	74.56	77.44	74.53	75.14	0.06^{NS}	0.06^{NS}	0.05^{NS}	0.05^{NS}	0.11^{NS}
3–5 years	96.47	91.28	91.48	89.87	91.56	96.50	91.33	91.58	89.95	91.63	0.01^{NS}	0.03^{NS}	0.04^{NS}	0.03^{NS}	0.04^{NS}
c) Mid-Arm circumference(cm)															
1–3 years	13.83	13.67	14.50	13.46	13.75	13.80	13.63	14.31	13.45	13.70	0.06^{NS}	0.07^{NS}	0.74^{NS}	–	0.22^{NS}
3–5 years	14.50	14.77	14.50	14.23	14.43	14.20	14.67	14.40	14.19	14.32	0.77^{NS}	0.44^{NS}	0.32^{NS}	0.13^{NS}	0.63^{NS}

NS : Not significant

The results of the family are comparable with the results reported by NNMB (1990-92) for the same age groups of rural Andhra Pradesh.

Body Mass Index (BMI)

Distribution of women according to their BMI values are provided in Table 30,

The prevalence of the chronic energy deficiency (BMI < 18.5) was 21 per cent both in "peak" and "lean" seasons.

The proportion of women with normal BMI values (18.5-25) was found to be different with regard to small farm and landless labour families between the seasons. But overall no change was found between the seasons (42%).

Weight for Age

The nutritional grades of preschool children as per the Gomez classification is given in Table 31.

The proportion of preschool children with normal nutritional grades was 8 per cent during season and in lean season it was 7 per cent. These results are comparable with Nagamablleswari (1989) study in Rangareddy district of Andhra Pradesh which is also a drought prone district. The study reported that 8.5 per cent of preschool children were with normal nutritional grade.

The proportion of preschool children with mild malnutrition was 49 per cent during peak season and in lean season it was 46 per cent.

The highest proportion of "severe and moderate" forms of malnutrition which constitutes the 'high risk' group from the stand point of health was 43 per cent during peak season and in lean season it was 48 per cent.

Swaminathan's (1973) study on 1,700 refugees of Bangladesh in West Bengal camps, Srivastva *et al.* (1980) study in Jhansi district, Bhat *et. al* (1985) study on 200 children of Gangwa village, Hissar district and Nagamalleswari (1989) study in Ranga Reddy district, Andhra Pradesh also revealed that "severe and moderate" forms of malnutrition ranged from 30-65 per cent in the preschool children. The results of the present study are comparable with the above results.

Table 30 : Frequency Distribution of Women according to BMI*

(n=18 for LF, MF & SF, n=36 for LL, n=90 for OAF)

BMI	Peak Season					Lean Season					't' Value				
Classification	LF	MF	SF	LL	OAF	LF	MF	SF	LL	OAF	LF	MF	SF	LL	OAF
III degree CED < 16.0	–	–	–	–	–	–	–	1 (6)	1 (3)	2 (2)	–	–	1.06^{NS}	1.05^{NS}	1.35^{NS}
II degree 16.0 – 17.0	–	–	2 (11)	1 (3)	3 (3)	–	–	2 (11)	–	2 (2)	–	–	–	1.05^{NS}	0.43^{NS}
I degree CED 17.0 – 18.5	2 (11)	4 (22)	5 (28)	5 (14)	16 (18)	2 (11)	4 (22)	4 (22)	5 (14)	15 (16)	–	–	0.42^{NS}	–	0.18^{NS}
Low normal 18.5 – 20.0	4 (22)	4 (22)	2 (11)	12 (33)	22 (24)	4 (22)	4 (22)	2 (11)	13 (36)	23 (26)	–	–	–	0.27^{NS}	0.31^{NS}
Normal 20-.0–25.0	12 (67)	10 (56)	8 (44)	17 (47)	47 (52)	12 (67)	10 (56)	8 (44)	16 (44)	46 (51)	–	–	–	0.26^{NS}	0.13^{NS}
Over-weight (I degree obese) 25.0 – 30.0	–	–	1 (6)	1 (3)	2 (2)	–	–	1 (6)	1 (3)	2 (2)	–	–	–	–	–
Obese > 30	–	–	–	–	–	–	–	–	–	–	–	–	–	–	–

(Figures within parentheses indicate percentage) NS : Not significant, *BMI : Body Mass Index = weight (kg)/height^2 (m)

Table 31 : Frequency distribution of Pre-school Children According to Gomez Classification*

(n=18 for LF, MF & SF, n=36 for LL, n=90 for OAF)

Gomez	*Peak Season*					*Lean Season*					*'t' Value*				
Classification	*LF*	*MF*	*SF*	*LL*	*OAF*	*LF*	*MF*	*SF*	*LL*	*OAF*	*LF*	*MF*	*SF*	*LL*	*OAF*
Normal > 90%	3 (17)	2 (11)	2 (11)	0	7 (8)	2 (11)	2 (11)	2 (11)	0	6 (7)	0.52_{NS}	–	–	–	0.25_{NS}
Mild malnutrition 75%–90%	14 (78)	9 (50)	10 (56)	11 (31)	44 (49)	15 (83)	8 (44)	10 (56)	8 (22)	41 (46)	0.38_{NS}	0.36_{NS}	–	0.87_{NS}	0.40_{NS}
Moderate malnutrition 60%–75%	1 (6)	7 (39)	5 (28)	23 (64)	36 (40)	1 (6)	8 (44)	5 (28)	24 (67)	38 (42)	–	0.30_{NS}	–	0.27_{NS}	0.27_{NS}
Severe malnutrition < 60%	0	0	1 (6)	2 (3)	3 (3)	0	0	1 (6)	4 (11)	5 (6)	–	–	–	$0.,76_{NS}$	0.97_{NS}

(Figures within parentheses indicate percentage.) NS : Not significant, *Weight for age (% of NCHS Standards)

The incidence of protein-energy-malnutrition (PEM), as measured by the number of children which mild or moderate levels of severity on the Gomez scale was not significantly different in all the categories of farming groups studied between the seasons.

Compared to small farm size groups, there was less seasonal variation in the proportion of preschool children with moderate and severe malnutrition among the large farm households (Table 33). The variation was sharpest in the lean period. This suggests that the children of less affluent households are more prone to seasonal malnutrition than those from more affluent households.

From the above observation, it is clear that, the percentage of children suffering from mild to moderate degree of malnutrition and severe malnutrition were higher than the figures obtained by NNMB (1990-92) in rural Andhra Pradesh. It shows the effect of dry spells on the nutritional status of the preschool children in these dryland districts.

The nutritional status of women was more or less similar to that of children's nutritional status. The farming group having higher proportion of women with chronic energy deficiency showed higher prevalence of malnourished children.

Though significant reduction in the nutrient consumption was observed in all the four categories of families in lean season compared to peak season (Table-28 & 29), corresponding decrease in nutritional status was not noticed in lean season compared to peak season. This may be because nutritional status of an individual is not dependent on nutrient intake alone, but there are multi-factors responsible for it.

Clinical Assessment

The frank nutritional deficiencies observed among women of child bearing age and preschool children (1-5 years) in different categories of farming groups are given in Table 32,

The nutritional deficiency symptoms observed among women and preschool children were anaemia, vitamin 'B' complex deficiency, including thiamine & riboflavin and vitamin A deficiency. In preschool children in addition to those, symptoms of protein energy malnutrition were also observed.

Table 32 : Frequency distribution of Women and Pre-school Children According to Prevalence of Nutritional Deficiency Signs

(n=60 for LF, MF & SF, n=120 for LL, n=300 for OAF)

Sl. No. Nutritional deficiency	Peak Season					Lean Season					't' Value				
	LF	MF	SF	LL	OAF	LF	MF	SF	LL	OAF	LF	MF	SF	LL	OAF
1. Marasmus	0	0	1 (1.67)	2 (1.67)	3 (1.00)	0	0	1 (1.67)	2 (1.67)	3 (1.00	–	–	–	–	–
2. Kwashiorkar	0	0	1 (1.67)	1 (0.83)	2 (0.67)	0	0	1 (1.67)	1 (0.83)	2 (0.67)	–	–	–	–	–
3. Anaemia															
a) Women	4 (6.67)	5 (8.33)	6 (10.00)	12 (10.00)	27 (9.0)	4 (6.67)	5 (8.33)	7 (11.67)	15 (12.50)	31 (10.33)	–	–	0.29^{NS}	0.61^{NS}	0.55^{NS}
b) Pre-school children	1 (1.67)	2 (3.33)	3 (5.00)	6 (5.00)	12 (4.00)	2 (3.33)	4 (6.67)	5 (8.33)	10 (8.33)	21 (7.00)	0.58^{NS}	0.84^{NS}	0.73^{NS}	1.03^{NS}	1.61^{NS}
4. Vitamin β-complex deficiency															
i) Thiamine															
a) Women	0	0	0	0	0	0	0	0	0	0					
b) Pre-school children	0	0	0	0	0	0	0	0	0	0					
ii) Riboflavin															
a) Women	3 (5.00)	5 (8.33)	5 (8.33)	11 (9.17)	24 (8.00)	2 (3.33)	4 (6.67)	4 (6.67)	9 (7.50)	19 (6.33)	0.46^{NS}	0.35^{NS}	0.35^{NS}	0.47^{NS}	0.79^{NS}
b) Pre-school children	4 (6.67)	6 (10.00)	8 (13.33)	15 (12.5)	33 (11.00)	3 (5.))	4 (6.67)	6 (10.00)	11 (9.17)	24 (8.00)	0.39^{NS}	0.66^{NS}	0.57^{NS}	0.83^{NS}	1.25^{NS}

(Contd.)

Table 32 : (Contd.)

(n=60 for LF, MF & SF, n=120 for LL, n=300 for OAF)

Sl. No.	Nutritional deficiency	Peak Season					Lean Season					't' Value				
		LF	MF	SF	LL	OAF	LF	MF	SF	LL	OAF	LF	MF	SF	LL	OAF
5.	Vitamin A deficiency															
	a) Women	0	0	1 (1.67)	0	1 (0.33)	0	0	1 (1.67)	0	1 (0.33)	–	–	–	–	–
	b) Pre-school children	1 (1.67)	2 (3.33)	2 (3.33)	5 (4.17)	10 (3.33)	1 (1.67)	2 (3.33)	2 (3.33)	4 (3.33)	9 (3.00)	–	–	–	0.34^{NS}	0.23^{NS}

(Figures within parentheses indicates percentage.)

NS : Not significant

Protein Calorie Malnutrition

The incidence of Marasmus in preschool children studied was 1.0 per cent in both peak and lean seasons and it is slightly higher than the results reported by NNMB (1990-92). However, the prevalence was higher among the small farm and landless labour groups, indicating the lower nutritional status of the groups.

The incidence of kwashiorkor in preschool children studied was 0.67 per cent in peak as well as in lean season indicating no seasonal difference. According to NNMB 1983-84 reports, the incidence of kwashiorkar was 0.3% among preschool children in rural Andhra Pradesh. The incidence of kwashiorkar was not observed in the large farm and medium farm groups. Whereas in the case of landless labour and small farm groups prevalence of kwashiorkar was slightly higher, compared to the NNMB values.

Anaemia

The increase in the prevalence of anaemia in lean season over the peak season was not significant in both women and preschool children of the four categories of families.

Vitamin 'B' Complex Deficiency

Thiamine deficiency: There were no frank signs of thiamine deficiency either among women or preschool children in all the groups studied in both the seasons indicating sufficient consumption of cereals and millets.

Riboflavin Deficiency

Prevalence of riboflavin deficiency symptoms was lower in lean season compared to peak season in both women and preschool children (Table-24). This was because of increased consumption of coarse grains in the lean season, compared to peak season. However, the difference between the seasons was not significant.

The per cent prevalence of riboflavin deficiency in the present study was higher compared to NNMB (1990-92) reports (6.2% for the preschool children) indicating the lowered consumption of milk and other protective foods rich in riboflavin.

Vitamin A Deficiency

The most common symptoms of vitamin A deficiency such as xerosis, bitot's spot and night were noted in the study.

In the case of women, the prevalence of vitamin A deficiency symptoms noticed in both the seasons was very low i.e. 0.33 per cent. Only in one woman of small farm household vitamin A deficiency was observed.

Prevalence of vitamin A deficiency symptoms among preschool children in peak season was 3.33 per cent and it reduced slightly to 3.0 per cent in lean season. A slight increase in the symptoms was observed in the case of landless labour families during the lean season (Table-32). The reported values of vitamin A deficiency symptoms by the NNMB for preschool children was slightly lower (1%) as compared with the present study.

The prevalence of the clinical nutritional deficiency symptoms observed were indirectly related to the land holding size in the four categories of families. Higher prevalence of the deficiency symptoms was observed in the present study as compared to the NNMB (1990-92) reported values in rural Andhra Pradesh, indicating the low consumption of protective foods such as milk, fruits, vegetables and fleshy foods which was very conspicuous during recurring droughts in these drought prone areas.

It can be concluded that there was slight increase in the incidence of deficiency symptoms, which was not significantly different either among women or preschool children of the four categories of families between the two seasons (Table-32).

5

Summary and Conclusions

Food security is a basic social objective and a sensitive policy issue. The present study was carried out in Ananthapur, a drought prone district of Andhra Pradesh to assess the coping mechanisms adapted by landless labour, small, medium and large farm households for food security and their nutritional status.

The general information of the selected families, having atleast one women of child bearing age and one preschool child (1-5 years), from the eight selected villages of the four mandals, was enumerated, by a pretested structured schedule. A total of 300 families were covered and two rounds of survey was conducted to understand difference in mechanisms operating between 'peak' and 'lean' seasons by interview method using a structured and pretested schedule specifically designed for the study.

The coping mechanisms adapted for food security by the households were as follows:

1. Food Production Based Coping Mechanisms

   a) ***Land Based Coping Mechanisms***

   Better options : Intercrop adjustments of cropped area, use of Farm yard manure, fertilisers, pesticides and weedicides; use of seed treatment procedures, use of hybrid or improved seeds, use of canal or tank water, well or borewell water and use of list irrigation method for irrigation purpose and seeking support from state agriculture department.

Hard option : Shrinking of net sown area

b) *Livestock Based Coping Mechanisms*

Better options: Animal rearing, rug weaving with sheep wool and seeking support from state veterinary department.

Frugal options: Foraging in common property

Hard options: Reduction in livestock owned due to selling, gifting and abandoning.

2. Employment, Economic and Income generation based coping mechanisms

Better options: Engaging in different non-farm occupations, working on small trades during off season and participating in welfare programmes.

Frugal option : Remittances from parents and relatives.

Hard options: Postponement of acquisition of all consumer durables, curtailment in the expenditure on all food & non-food items, institutional or private borrowing, accepting to work for low wages almost half to that of peak season wages, employing children, borrowing or begging grain/money.

3. Asset based coping mechanisms

Better options: Deepening of wells and digging well or bore well.

Hard options: Liquidation of Farm and Non-Farm assets by mortgaging or selling.

4. Food procurement based coping mechanism

Better options: Options to work for kind, sending children to AWC, procuring cheaper quality foods, collecting forest produce for food and generation of income and procuring unconventional foods.

Hard options: Decrease in procuring the foods grown or produced in own farms and PDS in lean season, decrease in purchasing foods by paying cash and increase in purchasing foods on loan.

5. Food storage based coping mechanisms

Better options: Storing staples, storing tamarind and red chillies for one year and storing the major produced and selling during economic crises.

6. Food preparation, consumption and distribution based coping mechanisms

Better options: Substitution of millets to rice and horsegram or cowpea to redgram.

Frugal option: Cooking only once in a day

Hard options: Selling the grain kept for seed purpose, curtailment in number of meals from 3 to 2 in a day, reducing meal size, curtailment in consumption of protective foods, curtailment in consumption of coffee or tea or diluting the milk, diluting the milk or giving coffee or tea instead of milk to the children, changing meal pattern by using more chutnies, salt, greenchillies, onion or korivikaram in place of vegetable curries, use of more puffed rice, curtailing work & activities to suppress hunger and forceful starvation.

7. Social based coping mechanisms

Better options: Curtailment in the use of intoxicants, cigarettes and pan.

Frugal options: Postponement of functions other than marriages, postponement or avoiding travel or travelling by walk and curtailment of recreation like cinema.

Hard options: Sending daughter-in-law along with children to parents house or children to grand parents house, avoiding guests, relatives friends, gifts, beggars and maintaining the secrecy of resources in the forests.

All the social activities involving expenditure got considerably reduced, minimising the social arena of live cycle itself, giving rise to life at low equilibrium of living to let the dry spell periods pass.

8. Health based coping mechanisms

Better options: Decrease in seeking health services from private clinics, increase in seeking health services from PHC, AWC, CHS and undergoing family planing operations at Government hospitals.

Frugal options: Seeking health services from native practitioners and home remedies.

Hard options: Seeking health services directly from medical shops, postponement of minor operations, postponement of treatment and not taking the treatment.

It was observed that a few of these mechanisms are found to be beneficial and can be encouraged whereas others are very harmful and necessary policy implications and immediate government interventions are required.

The mean intake of all foods were lower during lean season compared to peak season in both women and preschool children of the four categories of families. However, the intake of millets, GLVs and roots & tubes increased significantly in lean season. Except calories, protein and thiamine all the other nutrients i.e., fat, calcium, iron, riboflavin, β-carotene and ascorbic acid were deficient in both women and preschool children across all farm size groups in both seasons. In preschool children even the calorie and protein intake was below the requirement. Consumption of protein, fat and calcium showed significant decease across the seasons.

Significant difference was not observed in the nutritional, status of both women and preschool children across the two seasons as assessed by anthropometry measurements and clinical observation. The percentage of women and preschool children suffering from malnutrition was higher than the figures obtained by NNMB (1990-'92) for the same age group of rural Andhra Pradesh.

Conclusions and Implications

Intervention programme should be taken up in drought affected areas to prevent the nutritional status developing into worst forms of malnutrition and to increase the agricultural production.

Based on the results obtained in the present study, the following implications are suggested to uplift the living conditions of the families in drought prone areas to improve the food security system.

1. The long term strategy for achieving control on recurring drought rests in effective use of surface and ground water

and land resources for Agricultural production on one hand and provision of employment to labour force engaged in agricultural sector on the other.

2. It is essential to rural a global information and early warning system for food and agriculture, which monitors materiological conditions, harvests and food supplies, as well as market prices and other factors that effect food security.
3. The ceiling on land holding may have to be revised upward, specially in dryland, as the present limits were not yielding adequate income to maintain a reasonable standard of living. The excess land available can be distributed to the landless labourers.
4. Creating irrigation facilities on location specific dryland technology in these low productivity dryland areas is to be evolved on priority basis. Soil and moisture conservation activities through watershed approach can be intensified to sustain the cropped area. The intercropping system using cereal + legume is an insurance against drought and also a system of providing nutritious diet.
5. The integrated approach of both development of agriculture and livestock production need to be encouraged. Drought resistant crops as well as milch animal rearing need to be encouraged.
6. Community actions is necessary for the equal utilisation of common land property resources, as the same were taken advantage of more by the large farm households.
7. Minimum wages act was not followed in these acres. Protection of minimum wage act need to be followed strictly. One meal could be provided as a part of wages, specially for women and children.
8. As the cropping pattern intensity was so poor that agriculture did not provide required employment opportunities to these families, the coping strategies should focus more on non-farm activities in drought prone areas for generating income. There is need to stabilise the regular traditional occupations.
9. It was observed that about '43' types of income generating activities were undertaken in peak and lean season in these

areas. It is ideal to start rural industries on these area based activities to supplement their income.

10. The unemployed population were more in medium farm group than in small farm and landless labourer groups. Therefore, target oriented type of interventions should be discouraged. Emphasis also given to medium and large farmers.
11. Even though number of welfare programmes are existing, only 5-16 per cent of sample households received support from state agriculture and veterinary departments for increasing food production. Further Augmentation of ongoing welfare programmes may help the farmers for better survival strategies.
12. Effective implementation of welfare programmes focussing on non-farm activities is required to overcome food insecurity. Production of more profitable consumer goods should be encouraged through upgradation of skills and promotion of sales. However, caution must be exercised in implementing income generating activities, which consume more human energy and less returns.
13. Welfare and developmental programme such as JRY, RDT, YIP have contributed to food security in the study areas. However, at household level, the family has to take right decision to take advantage of the programmes and acquire adequate food and make it available to all members of the family. PDS can be expanded to include legumes, biscuits and infant foods, to mitigate protein inadequacy. DWCRA programme can be utilised for procuring biscuits and snacks for distribution through PDS. School feeding can be introduced in dryland areas.
14. The debt status of rural families reached as alarming stage even among large farm families. The solution to minimise the burden of indebtedness, lies in augmenting their income by taking up suitable and helpful occupations, specially in lean season with the assistance of institutional finance. Thrift and credit groups can be encouraged under DWCRA programme.
15. Implementation of Food stamps site practiced in some developed countries like Japan is beneficial to the poorer section

of people, by preventing them not to divert their earning towards other non-food expenditure like luxuries etc. It is advisable to follow the similar system in developing countries like India. Access to money or Food stamps during peak season will enable the people to procure foods adequately for lean season.

16. Food storage sufficiency can be increased by giving more ration through PDS during peak season, when the population has more purchasing power specially in drought prone regions, like the study areas. Millets can be distributed through PDS on subsidy during lean season. Education on appropriate storage structures and storage methods of different foods is required to improve the storage sufficiency index, by storing the foods available plenty in peak season for use in slack periods.

17. The variety of foods consumed is highly limited to cereal, groundnut, tamarind and chillies. Increasing productivity of millet, legumes and green leafy vegetables will help to ensure food security.

18. Forests and farm trees provide a vast array of foods which supply many essential nutrients especially at times when other food supplies are depleted. Plants like beer, palm, custard apple which are able to withstand drought, provide excellent sources of nutrition. Awareness about their cultivation and use need to be created.

19. Projects like way side agro-forestry such as planting of fruit trees along roads and common property resources could be taken up to supplement the food intake of the villagers.

20. A combination of nutrition activities including growth monitoring of the children and nutrition education using problem solving approaches have to be integrated into the credit sessions that women attend.

21. Drastic reduction in the pulse consumption levels was observed. With the ongoing distribution of the staple (cereals) and edible oil through the fair price shops, it is advisable that a minimum quantity of 40 g of pulse per day is supplied so that the quality of diets during drought does not suffer. In otherwords, a family of 3 adults and 2 children (4 consumption units) can be supplied about 5 kg of pulse per month.

22. In view of the acute vitamin and mineral deficiencies in these villages, programmes to increase the production and consumption of drought resistant varieties of fruits and vegetables would seem appropriate.
23. Necessary media strategy has to be developed to bring about awareness on how to utilise their resources in a better way.
24. Nutrition education programmes have to be taken up in the area to improve nutritional security.
25. Above all constant and continuous monitoring of the on-going welfare programmes and effective implementation of the same will lead to increased food availability.

As long as poverty exists households will be unable to defend their level of food intake during a crisis. They will be dependent on outside assistance to survive, an assistance that usually comes only when severe damage had occurred. Therefore one must strive hard to enhance their endurance by ensuring food security at the household level as both production and consumption of food must take place at the household level. No matter how far reaching or effective government's intervention in the food sector may be, the ultimate responsibilities and penalties in the food system fall on people and their families and that a nation's food security situation is the summation of the prospects of individual households.

Scope for further research

Extension of the similar type of studies to the other drought prone areas will help to understand the information on area based coping mechanism; so that suitable indictors can be developed to target food aid to the food insecure.

Bibliography

Acharya K. T. and Mitra R. (1974), Some highlights of food patterns in South India. Proceedings of Nutrition Society of India 18:27-28.

Achaya K.T. (1978), Visible and invisible fat consumption in India and the influence of region, income and age - (a) Availability of consumption of visible fat. *Indian Journal of Nutrition and Dietetics 15:120-128.*

Agarwal B. (1990), Social security and family : Coping with seasonality and calamity in Rural India. *Journal of Peasant Studies 17: 3 : 341-412.*

Agarwal R P. (1992), Tackling Drought thro' soil and water management (a study of north-west India measures) *Kurukshetra* Dec : 29-38.

Alderman H, Garcia M. (1993), Poverty, household food security, and nutrition in rural Pakistan, Research Report 96, International Food Policy Research Institue, Washington D.C.

All Indian Coordinated Research Project in Foods and Nutrition - Report of the study on Food and Nutrition Situation of Rural Families in seven Agro-climatic zones of Andhra Pradesh (1992-1993), Andhra Pradesh Agricultural University, Hyderabad.

Andherson P P. (1981), Energy Cropping and Food, Reprinted, *IFPRI Report*: 16, 17.

Annual Report, 1989-90, Department of Agriculture, Government of India, Report of the National Commission on Agriculture, 1976 (abridged), Ministry of Agriculture, Government of India, New Delhi.

Anuradha N. (1990), Impact of rural women's income on Food and nutrient intake and nutritional status of families, in Moinabad mandal, Rangareddy District, Andhra Pradesh, *M.Sc. thesis, Andhra Pradesh Agricultural University, Hyderabad.*

Anurag Chaturvedi (1983), Food and Nutrient intake of population in groundnut cultivating areas, studies on utilisation of groundnut in Dryland region of A.P. and nutritional evaluation of Raw and Processed groundnuts of selected varities. *Thesis submitted to Andhra Pradesh Agricultural University, Hyderabad.*

Arora C.L. (1982-83), Sheep farming in Drylands of Bundelkhand. *Indian Farming 32 (5): 27-32.*

Asthurkar B.W. and Doele C.D. (1977), Nutritional status of farm families in Prabhani District, Maharastra. *Indian Journal of Agricultural Economics 32 : 105.*

Bai K I, Sastry V. N. and Reddy C. (1984), A comparative study of feeding pattern of infants in rural and urban areas. *Indian Journal of Paediatrics 48 : 277–80.*

Basu B. (1992), Coping with natural disasters (preventive measures). *Kurukshetra Dec : 29-31.*

Bhal C. M. and Saroj D. (1985), Nutritional status of preschool children in Gangua village of Hissar district. The *Indin Journal of Nutrition and Dietetics 22 : 206.*

Bidinger P. D. (1983), Agricultural and socio-economic determinants of human nutrition in the semi-arid tropics of India. *Ph.D. thesis, Cornell University,* Ithaca New York, U.S.A.

Bidinger P. D., Walker T. S., Sarkar B., Ram Murthy and Babu P. (1990), Economic, health and nutritional consequences of the Mid-1980s drought on a tank irrigated, Deccan village in South India, Resource management prog. economics group. Progress *Report - 98, ICRISAT, International Crops Research Institute for the Semi Arid Tropics.*

Biellik and Hendeson P. L. (1981), Mortality, nuritional status and dietary conditions in a food deficit region. North Terso District, Ugana, *Ecology of Food and Nutrition 11 : 163-70.*

Biswanger P. H. and Braun J. V. (1984), Technological change and commercialization in agriculture. *The effect on the poor 6, 1 : 57-79.*

Bovis H. E. and Haddad J. L. (1990), Effects of Agricultural commercialisation on land tenure, household resource allocation and nutrition in the Phillippines : IFPRS : 9-65.

Braun J. V. (1989), Irrigation technology and commercialisation of rice in Gambia : Effects on income and nutrition. *IFPRI Research Report* 75 : 9-103.

Braun J. V. (1989), Non-traditional Export Crops in Guatemala and the effects on production, *Income and Nurition 73 : 11-89.*

Braun J. V. (1989), Commercialization of Agriculture under population pressure and the effects on production, consumption and nutrition, Rwanda : 11-95.

Braun J .V., Puetz D. and Webb P. (1989), Technological change in rice and commercialisation of agriculture in a West African setting : effects on production, consumption and nutrition. Research Report 75, Washington D C, International Food Policy Research Institute.

Braun J. V. and Lorch R. P. (1992), Income sources and diversification strategies of the malnourished rural poor. *Quarterly Journal of International Agriculture* 31 (1) : 36 - 54.

Braun J .V., Teklu T. and Webb P. (1992), *Labour* intensive public works for food security in Africa : past experience and future potential. Reprint No. 247, IFPRI 131 (1); 19-32.

Braun J. V., Howarth Bovis Shubh Kumar, Rajul Pandya and Lorch (1992), Improving food security of the poor, Concept, Policy and Programmes, *IFPRI Reports.*

Census of India, (1981), Series -2 (Andhra Pradesh) by S.S. Jaya Rao-Paper - 1 of 1981. Supplement Provisional Population totals.

Census of India (1991) Series -1, Brief Analysis of primary census Abstract - Registrar General and Census Commissioner, India.

Census Book (1994), Directorate of Economics and Statistics, Government of Andhra Pradesh, Hyderabad.

Chandel S. R. S. (1993), *A handbook of Agricultural Statistics*, Achal Prakashan Mandir, 117/574, Pandunagar, Kanpur.

Chandrasekhara Rao N., Shareef and Srinivasulu (1992), Impact of commercialisation of Agriculture and Farm Employment in Prakasam district of Andhra Pradesh. *Agriculture Situation in India XLVII 2 : 105-110.*

Chaudhary R. (1988), Adequacy of child dietary intake relative to that of other family member. *Food and Nutritional Bulletin* 10(2): 26-35.

Chauhan S. P. (1994), Employment and Food Security through Employment Assurance Scheme. *Yojana*, December 31:11-13.

Chittemma Rao K. and Vimala V. (1987), Devlopment of women and children in Rural areas (DWCRA) of Andhra Pradesh - A review. *Journal of Rural Development 6 : 180-85.*

Daulay H. S. (1984), Increasing and stabilising crop production on drylands 34 (10) : 23-25.

Devadas R. P., Rajalakshmi R. and Kaveri R. (1980), Influency of family income and parent's education on the nutritional status of preschool children. *The Indian Journal of Nutrition and Dietetics,* 17:237-243.

Devadas R. P., Usha T. M., Shankari L and Geetha P. (1980), Diet nutrition survey of a village community in South India. *Journal of Nutrition and Dietetics* 2 : 83.

Devadas R. P., Premkumari S., Geeta G. and Aruna C. (1983), Prevalence of nutritional and non-nutritional diseases among 0-6 years old childrn and their nutritional status. *Indian Journal of Nutrition and Dietetics* 20(1) : 1

Distribution of household and persons by monthly per capita expenditure class for different calorie intake levels, NSS 38th Round (Jan. 1983-Dec. 1983), Sarnekshana (1994), 58th issue, volume XVII No. 3:41–87, National Sample Survey Organisation, Department of Statistics, Ministry of Planning, Government of India.

Donaldson G. (1983), A global approach to household food security. Food frameworks for analysis and action policy by Chalres K Mann, Barbara, Huddlestun. Indian University Press, Bloomington : 117-25.

Dreze and Jean (1988), 'Famine Prevention in India', DEP No. 3, The Development Economics Research Programme, London: London School of Economics.

Edmundson W. C. and Edmundson S. A. (1988), Food intake and work allocation of male and female farmers in an impoverished Indian village. *Journal of Nutrition* 60 : 433-39.

Engel E. (1985), Diet productions and consumption, Verhaltnissedes Kenigriechs Sachsen, Originally in Zietschriftdes Statisticher Bureaus des Koniglich Sachsischer Ministerium des Innerer: 8 & 9.

Faaland J. (1991), 'Strategies for Agricultural Research and Technology Transfer related to Food security'. Towards a new Agricultual Revolution; Research, Tech. Transfer and application for food security in Africa, IFPRI/ISNAR: 36-53.

FAO (1992), Food and Nutrition : Creating a well fed world, edited by Edourd Suomo, Director General, FAO of the United Nations pp. 2-8.

Finau (1985), Food consumption patterns during a drought in Tonga. *Newzealand Medical Journal 98* : 783 : 599-600.

Food Security, (1992) *Food, Nutrition and Agriculture*, 2, 4 : 2- 48.

Forestry and Food Security - FAO Forestry Paper 90, Food and Agricultural Organisation of the United Nations, Rome (1989): 66-98.

Frengley G. A. G. and Johnson W. E. (1992), Financial stress and consumption expectations among farm households : New Zealand's experience with economic liberalisation. *Journal of Agricultural Economics* 43(1) : 14-26.

Gadgil O. R. (1942), Poona Socio-economic Survey Part I Gokhale Institute of Politics and Economics, Poona : 288.

Gahukap R. T. (1994), The Problem of Food Security. *Kisan World* 21 (3) : 43-45.

Govan J. D. and Chandrasekhara I. (1979), The Impact of public distribution of food grain on food consumption and welfare in Srilanka. *IFPRI Report* 13 : 11.

Geervani P., Anuradha P., Geetha Sailaja P., Sandharyakumari R. and Nageswara Rao G. (1983), The consequence of development programme on the nutrient intake and nutritional status of vulnerable segments of population in Andhra Pradesh, Journal of Rural Development 2(6) : 571–80.

George P. S. (1985), A study of some aspects of procurement and distribution of food grains in India. *Report on Coarse for Developmental Studies*, Tivandrum.

Ghal O. P., Ghandial S. N., Kapoor S., Jaiswal V. N. and Sinclair S. (1979), Nutritional assessment of preschool children of rural community. *Indian Journal of Medical Research* 5:1621-628.

Gillespite S. R. and Mason J. B. (1991), Nutrition Relevant Actions: Some Experiences from the Eighties and lessons for the Nineties, ACC/SCN State of the Art Series, Nutrition Policy Discussion Paper No. 10, United Nations, Geneva.

Gomez F., Galvan R., Cravioto J. and frenck S. (1955), Malnutrition in infancy and childhood with special reference to Kwashiorkor. *Adavances in Paediatrics* 7:131-36.

Gomez F., Gralvan R., Frank S., Canoto J., Chavez and Vasonez J. (1956), Mortality in second and third degree malnutrition. *Journal of Tropical Pediatrics* 2 : 77-83.

Gopaldas T. and Seshadri S. (1989), Nutritional Monitoring and Assessment.

Gopalan C. and Raghavan K. (1971), Nutrition Atlas of India. National Insitute of Nutrition, ICMR, India.

Gopalan C., Rama Sastri B. V. and Balasubrahmanian S. C. (1991), Nutritive value of Indian foods, revised and updated by B S Narasinga Rao, Y. G. Deosthale and K. C. Pant National Insitute of Nutrition, ICMR, Hyderabad, India.

Government of India (1985), National Sample Survey 32nd Round. A Note on the Second Quinquennial Survey on Consumer Expenditure : 13-19.

Govindaiah M. G., Jayashankar M. R. and Rai A. V. (1986), Animal husbandry in dryland farming areas. *Indian Farming* 36 (2): 31-32.

Gupta D. B. (1973), *Consumption pattern in India*. Tata McGraw-Hill Publishing Company Limited, Bombay, New Delhi.

Gupta S. P. (1976), Statistical methods, sampling and tests of significance. Sulthan Chand and Sons Publishers, 4792/23, Daryaganj, New Delhi - 11002 : A-3.2 to A-3.48.

Gupta M. Jain and Singh (1978), Nutritional Status of Urban and Rural Preschool children in West Rajasthan. *Indian Journal of Paediatics* 5:247.

Gupta S. P. (1983), *Practical Statistics.* Chand S. & Company Limited, Ram Nagar, New Delhi.

Hamill P. V. V., Drizd T. A., Johnson C. L., Reed R. B., Roche A. F. and Moore, WIM (1979) Physical growth: National centre for Health statistics percentiles, *American Journal of clinical Nutrition,* 32, 607-29.

Handbook of Statistics, Ananthapur District 1990-91.

Handbook of Statistics, Ananthapur District 1991-92 and 1992-93, compiled by chief Planning Officer, Ananthapur.

Handbook of Statistics, Andhra Pradesh 1993094, Directorate of Economics and Statistics, Government of Andhra Pradesh, Hyderabad.

Hanumantha Rao D., Satyanarayana K. and Gowrinath Sastry J. (1976), Growth Pattern of Well Hyderabad Preschool children. *The Indian Journal of Medical Research* 64:629-38.

Hanumantha Rao D. (1986), Assessment of growth and development, lead paper presented at the National Level Symposium organised by the Department of Home Science, School of Biological and Earth Sciences, Sri Venkateswara University, Tirupati, November 11-14, 1986.

Hassan N. and Ahmed K. (1983), Studies on food and nutrient intake by rural population of Bangladesh : comparison of intake of 1962-64, 75-76 and 81-82. *Ecology of Foods and Nutrition* 18 : 143-58.

Hassan N., Huda N. and Ahmed K. (1985), Seasonal patterns of food intake in Rural Bangladesh : Its impact on Nutritional Status. *Ecology of Foods and Nutrition* 17 : 175-86.

Hossain M. (1988), Credit for allevation of rural poverty : The Grameena Bank in Bangladesh, Research Report 65, International Food Policy Research Institute, Washington, D.C.

Hunger and "Surplus" Food: A strange Co-existence, Food for

Development. *Newsletter of the World Food Programme in India* 3 : 38-39 (Oct. 1993).

ICMR (1990) Report of the Expert group of the Indian Council of Medical Research, Nutrition requirement and Recommended Dietary Allowances for Indians, ICMR, New Delhi.

Inder Pal Singh (1986), Rural Income Distribution - An Analytical study of Punjab. B.R. Publishing Corporation : 100.

Indian Agriculture in Brief (1988), 23rd Edition Directorate of Economics and Statistics, Department of Agriculture and Cooperation, Ministry of Agriculture, Government of India.

IFPRI Reports (1988), Food consumption and nutrition policy programme research results 30-38.

India, Ministry of Planning, Central Statistical Organisation, *Second Seminar on Social Statistics, February* 4-6, 1988. New Delhi.

India, Office of the Register General, Vital Statistics, Division, Sample Registeration System, 1971, 1981-1986.

Imminic M. D. C. and Alarcon J. A. (1992), Household food security and crop diversification among small holder farmers is Guatemala; Can maize and beans save the day? Household income, food availability and commercial crop production by small holder farmers in the western highlands of Guatemala, Econ. Dev. Cultural Change (In Press).

Islam N. (1988), Linkages between Agriculture and the Overall Economy. The changing Dynamics of Global Agricultur, Seminar/Workshop on Research policy implications for National Agricultural Research Systems, DSE/ZELV Feldofing, Germany: 22-28, 67-87.

James W. P. T. Anna Ferro-Luzzi and Water Low J. C. (1988), Definition of Chronic Energy Deficiency in adults. European Journal of Clinical Nutrition 42:969-81.

Jawahar Rojgar Yojana, Manual, Government of India, Ministry of Agriculture, Department of Rural Development, New Delhi.

Jellifee D. B. (1966), The Assessment of the Nutritional Status of the Community. Monograph Series 53, Geneva W. H. O.

Jodha (1975), Mascarenhas (1983) and Binswanger (1984) Drought induced instability of food intakes and nuritional levels. Research studies conducted by ICRISAT, Hyderabad.

Jodha N. S. (1989), Drought Management. The Farmers' strategies and their policy implications. *Paper presented at the National Workshop on Management of Agriculture and Cooperatives, Government of India.*

John M. (1981), Food security in the Sahel : variable import heavy, grain reserves and foreign exchange assistance. International Food Policy Research Institute, *Research Report* 26, Washington, D.C.

John W. H. (1981), Food security failing the test - some comments on food, report prepared for world food day, Oct. 16, 1981, IFPRI, Washington, D.C. : 2-3.

Josling T. and Barichello R. (1984), International trade and World Food Security. The role of developed countries since the World Food Conference, *Food Policy* 9 (4): 317-27.

Kahlon A. S. and Johl S. S. (1963), Levels of living in rural areas of the Punjab. Indian Journal of Agricultural Economics **18:243.**

Kakkar S., Hooda A., Jain R., Kapoor A. C. and Voidya Sagar (1987), Nutritional Status of Pre-school children in rural Hissar. ***Indian*** *Journal of Nutrition and Dietetics* 24:204.

Kalla J. C. and Purohit M. L. (1987), Coping strategies of households in high risk arid environment : A case study of drought in arid districts of Western Rajasthan. *Paper presented at Workshop on sustainable development of high risk environments*, IIM, Ahmedabad; 9-12 March, 1992, 1-13.

Kanwar J. S. (1982), Managing soil resources to meet the challenge of hunger. Indian Farming 32(4): 3-5.

Kanwar J.S. (1989), Chairman's remarks in symposium on "Drought and Nutrition". *Proceedings of Nutrition Society of India* 35:57.

Karanth G. K. (1993), Farmers survival strategies in drought prone areas: A case study of a village in Chitradurga District, Karnataka. Agricultural Situation in India March 1993: 905-8.

Kennedy F. (1987), "Income and Nutritional effects of the commercialisation of Agriculture in South western Kenya", IFPRI, Res. Report 9-59.

Kennedy E. (1989), The effects of sugarcane production on Food security. Health and Nutrition in Kenya, IFPRI 79: 9-55.

Kennedy E. and Oniango R. (1990), Health and Nutrition effects of sugar cane production in South-Western Kenya. *Food and Nutrition Bulletin* 12 (4) : 261-267.

Kennedy E. and Hodded L. (1992), Food security and nutrition. Food Policy 237, IFPRI, 17(1) : 2-6.

Koester U. (1986), Regional Co-operation to improve food security in Southern and Eastern African countries, *Research Report* 53, IPPRI, Washington, D.C.

Krishnamachai K. A. V. R., Pralhad Rao N. and Visweswara Rao K. (1974), Food and Nutritional Situational situation in the drought affected areas of Maharastra - a survey and recommendations. *The Indian Journal of Nutrition and Dietetics* 11:20-27.

Krishnamachari K. A. V. R. (1989), Nutrition studies during drought - studies in the Western Rajasthan. *Proceedings of Nutrition Society of India* 35 : 82-87.

Krishna G. V. S. R., Yadav M. D. and Kalla C. J. (1985), Impact of five year plans on the productivity of dryland cereals in Western Rajasthan. *Agricultural Situation in India*, December 1985 : 785-788.

Kumar S. (1995), Workshop on Nutrition Situation, National Nutrition Policy (NNP) and National Plan of Action for Nutrition (NPAN), Government of India, Department of Women and Child Development, New Delhi.

Lawrenece J. H. and Boris H. E. (1990), "Effects of Agricultural Commercialisation Land Tenure, household Resource allocatio and Nutrition in the Phillippines" IFPRS, *Res. Report* 9-65.

Lidislav H. (1980), Effect of drought on tribal economy in western part of Sudan Disaster 4 (1) : 65-71.

Lincolin C. Chen, Chowdhury A. K. M. and Sandra L. Huffman (1979), Seasonal dimensions of energy protein malnutrition in Rural Bangaldesh : The Role of Agriculture, Dietary Practices and infection. Ecology of Food and Nutrition 8 : 175-87.

Livestock Census (1987), Bureau of Economics and Statistics, Government of Andhra Pradesh.

Lunven P. (1982), The nutritional consequences of Agricultural and rural development projects. *Food Nutrition Bulletin 4* : 17-22.

Maheswari V. C. and Peramma D. (1970), A study of the factors affecting food habits of employees in Sri venkateswara University, Tirupathi and their effect on the nutritional status of children (2.5-7.5 years) and lactating mothers. *Thesis submitted to S. V University cited from monograph series, Foods and Nutrition*, ed. Dr. P.R. Reddy, Tirupathi.

Martha Alter Chen (1991), Coping with seasonality and drought. Sage Publications Indian Private Limited, New Delhi 110048.

Mellor W. J. (1987), Links between Technology, Agricultural Development, Economic Growth and *Trade Creation* 136: 19-23.

Memorandum on drought situation in Andhra Pradesh 1987-88 *Revenue Department*; Government of Andhra Pradesh.

Miladi S. and Pellett L. P. (1986), Food and nutrition in the middle East and North Africa. Food Science and Human Nutrition, Pergamon Press, New York, Oxford Toranto, Sydney, Frankfurt : 132-75.

Miller D. S. and Hold J. F. J. (1975), The Ethiopian famine, Proc. Nutr. Soc. 34 : 167-72.

Ministry of Food and Civil Supplies, Food and Nutrition Board, Department of Food, National Workshop on Dietary and Nutritional Guidelines for Food and Agriculture Planning, October 4-6, 1989, New Delhi.

Mujamdar Rahman M. (1978), The causes and effects of famine in the rural population. *A report from Bangladesh. Ecology of Food and Nutrition* 7 : 99-102.

Muranjan (1991). Impact of 1987-88 droughts on the economic conditions of rural poor in Maharastra. Agricultural Situation in India XLVI, 9 : 677–81.

Nagamalleswari E. (1989), A study on nutritional status of vulnerable segments of population in a drought affected area in Andhra Pradesh. *M.Sc. thesis submitted to Andhra Pradesh Agricultural University, Hyderabad.*

Naidu V. T. (1985), Causes and impact of drought (an empirical study of Ananthaplur district of Andhra Pradesh. Agricultural Situation in India XL 6 : 521-24.

NARP Southern Regional Workshop, University of Agricultural Sciences, Bangalore 5-6 Januray, 1995 on *National Agricultural Research Project* - Profile and Achievements by APAU, Rajendranagar, Hyderbad pp. 73-82.

National Agricultural Research Project, High Altitude x Tribal Area zone, *Status Report - Volume 1*, APAU, RARS, Chinthapalli, Visakhapatnam district, December 1994, pp. 1-32.

National Bureau of Plant Genetics Resources - IARI Campus, New Delhi.

National Institute of Nutrition (1988), Diet and Nutrition during drought. Nutrition News 9(4).

National Nutrition Monitoring Bureau, *Report of Repeat Surveys* 1988-90, National Institute of Nutrition, ICMR, Hyderabad.

National Nutrition Policy (NNP) (1995), Workshop on Nutritional Situation, Government of India and Department of Women and Child Development, New Delhi.

NCHS Strandard Values (1983), Cited from measuring change in nutritional status guidelines for assessing the nutritional impact of supplementary feeding programme, for vulnerable groups. *World Health Organistion*, Geneva pp. 61-101.

Neela M. and Amitabha M. (1994), Rural women and food insecurity: What a food calender reveals. *Economic and Political Weekly* XXIX, 17 : 597-99.

Neuman C. G., Harishankar and Oberoi I. S. (1969), Nutritional and Anathropometric profile of young rural Punjabi children. *Indian Journal of Medical Research* 57:1122.

Neumann C., Trostle R., Baksh M., Ngare D. and Bwibo N. (1989), Household response to the impact of drought in Kenya. *Food and Nutrition Bulletin* Vol. II(2): 21-32.

NIN Annual Report (1987), Food and nutrition status of people in drought affected areas of the country 99-105.

NIN, NNMB, Interim Report of Repeat Survey, Phase-I, 1989.

NNNB (1980), Report for the year 1979 National Institute of Nutrition ICMR, Hyderabad.

NNMB (1981), Report for the year 1980 National Institute of Nutrition, ICMR, Hyderabad.

NNMB Report of the NNMB-NSSO Linked Survey 1983-84, NIN, ICMR, Hyderabad.

NNMB (1984), Report for the year 1983 NIN, ICMR, Hyderabad pp. 1-71.

NNMB, Interim report of repeat survey, Phaste-I (1988-89), NIN, Hyderabad (1989).

NNMB Annual Survey Report (1990-1992), NIN, ICMR, Hyderabad.

NNMB, Report of Urban Survey slums (1993-94), NIN, ICMR, Hyderabad.

NSS (1986) Design, concepts, definitions of procedures. Forty third round National sample survey organistion, Government of India, New Delhi.

Omawale and Joan C. and Leod M. C. (1984), Food consumption and poverty in rural Jamica. *Ecology of Food and Nutrition* 14 : 297-306.

Paramjit A., Miglani and Singh A. J. (1983), A comparative study on the nutrient intake among different income, occupation and family size categories in rural areas of Punjab. *Indian Journal of Nutrition and Dietetics* 30 : 344-46.

Payne P. and Lipton M. (1993), How third world rural households adapt to energy stress: The evidence and the issues, *Food Policy Review 2*, IFPRI, Washington, D.C.

Prahlad Rao N. Singh D. and Swaminathan M. C. (1969), Nutritional status of preschool children of rural communituies near Hyderabad city. *Indian Journal of Medical Research* 57(11): 2132-146.

Prahlad Rao N. and Gowrinath Sastri J., NIN, towards the implementation of a National Nutrition Policy in India. Pub. ICMR, 1986.

Prahlad Rao, Hanumantha Rao D. and Narasinga Rao B. S. (1987), Drought and Nutrition, *Nutrition News* 8:6.

Prahlad Rao, Hanumantha Rao D., Brahmam G. N. V., Gowrinath Sastry J., Vijaya Raghav N. K., Sathyanarayana K., Ramesware Sarma K. V., Meela J., Gal Reddy C. H., Sarad Kumar and Ravinranath (1989), Nutrition situation in drought affected states. *Proc. Nutrition Society of Indian* 35 : 64-75.

Pramila J. (1989), A study on the expenditure pattern and nutritional status of DWCRA Beneficiary Families inSrikakulam district, Andhra Pradesh. *M.Sc. thesis*, Andhra Pradesh Agricultual University, Hyderabad.

Pushpamma, P., Geervani P. and Usha Rani M. (1981), Food intake and nutrient adequacy of rural population of A.P., India. Human Nutrition : Applied Nutrition 36 : 293.

Pushpamma P., Geervani P. and Manoramma R. (1985), Food and nutrient intake of preschool and school children of the three regions of Andhra Pradesh. *Nutritional Reports International* (1985).

Radhakrishna R., Sudhakar Reddy S. and Gautam Kumar Mitra (1994), Rural labour markets in irrigated and dry zones of Andhra Pradesh, presented to the seminar on "work opportunities for all issues in policy, strategy programmes"; held in April, 1989. IASSI Quarterly, 9, 3 : 131–44.

Rajagopalan S. (1978), Seasonal dimensions of rural poverty. Tamilnadu Nutrition Project : A case study, July.

Rama Devi M. (1986), A comparative study of food and nutrient intake and nutritional status of population in sorghum and on sorghum eating population of Andhra Pradesh. *Thesis submitted to Andhra Pradesh Agricultural University*, Hyderabad.

Ramana R. and Reddy C. N. (1982), Consumption pattern of small farmers in Bangalore district. Mysore Journal of Agricultural Sciences 16 (2) : 203-8.

Ramaswamy C. (1988), Coping with floods and droughts. The Hindu Survey of Indian Agriculture : 65-67.

Ramnath T., Vijayaraghavan K. and Swaminathan M. C. (1983), Cereal-millet intake as an indicator of calorie adequacy. Nutrition Reports International 27(4):671-80.

Ranagaswamy P. (1992), The impact of droughts on rural economy in Haryana. *Agricultural Situation in India* 11 : 819-22.

Rao D. and Gowrinath Sastry (1976), Growth pattern of well to do Hyderabad preschool children. *Indian Journal of Medical Research* 6 : 629-38.

Rao, Hanumanth C. H., Ray S. K. and Subba Rao K. (1988), *Unstable Agriculture and Droughts*, New Delhi. Vikas Publishing House Private Limited.

Rao T. M. V. P., Sastry J. G. and Vijayaaraghavan (1974), Nutritional status of children in urban slums around Hyderabad city. *Indian Journal of Medical Research* 62 : 1492-98.

Reddy J. R. (1986), Why poverty continues? *Yojana* 30 : 20-21.

Reddy V., Prahlad Rao N., Gowrinath Sastry J. and Kashinath K. (1993), Nutrition trends in India, NIN, Hyderabad.

Reardon T., Matlon P. and Delgado C. (1988), Coping with household-level food security in drought affected areas of Burkina Faso, World Dev. 16:1065–74.

Reitsma H., Dietz T. and Haan L. D. (1992), A comparison of livelihood options and living conditions in five Semi Arid areas in Moracco, Kenya, Togo, Mexico and Spain.

Renu B. Patel (1989), Survey in Drought affected Tribal Areas, Proc. Nutrition Society of India 35:78-81.

Research Results, International Food Trade and Food Security Programm. IFPRI : 38-43.

Richards P. (1983), Coping with hunger - Hazard and experiment in an African rice farming system. Allen and Onwin Publishers Limited, 40 Museum Street, London, Won ILU UK (Boston), Sydney.

Robin J., Bellik P. and Henderson (1981), Mortality, Nutritional status and Diet during the famine in Karamoja. Ugana, Lancet 2:1330-33.

Robin J. B. and Henderson P. L. (1981), Mortality, Nutritional status and Dietary conditions in a food deficit region : North teso district, UGANEA, December 1980. *Ecology of Food and Nutrition* 11:163-70.

Rohini Devi M., Phadnis L. and Rama Rao (1990), Dietary pattern of malnourished Marathwada preschool childrn. *The Indian Journal of Nutrition and Dietetics* 27:115-23.

Rathur B. S., Mathur H. C. and Saxena S. (1975), Nutritional Anthropometry of 1000 children dwelling in slum areas of Jaipur compared to that of 500 children of the Elite. *Indian Journal of Pediatrics* 42 : 264-75.

Ryan J. G., Bidinger P. D., Prahlad Rao N. and Pushpamma P. (1984), The determinants of individual diets and nutritional status in six villages of Southern India, *Research Bulletin No. 7*, ICRISAT, Patancheru, A.P., India.

Sahay B. N. (1990), Chakriya Vikas Pranali - unique drought proofing. Kurukshetra, September 48-51.

Sailaja B. (1986), 'A comparative study of nutritional status of sorghum and non sorghum eating population of Andhra Pradesh'. *Thesis submitted to Andhra Pradesh Agricultural University*, Hyderabad.

Saila Kumari C. (1989), A comparative study of Food and Nutrient intake and Nutritional status of families with and without supplementary income of women in Rajendranager mandal, Rangareddy District, Andhra Pradesh. *M.Sc. thesis, Andhra Pradesh Agricultural University*, Hyderabad.

Sanghi U. (1964), Income, Expenditure and Consumption Pattern-A rural study - Jaipur District. *Economic Review*, New Delhi 16 : 19-25.

Schuftan C. (1979), 'Household purchasing-power deficit' a more operational indicator to express malnutrition. *Ecology of Food and Nutrition* 8 : 29-35.

Second Report on the World Nutrition Situation (1993), Volume II, country trends, methods and statistics, United Nations, *Nations Unies, administrative Committee on Coordination - Subcommittee on Nutrition.*

Sharma R. P. (1992), Role of Farm extension in Drought Management. *Agricultural Situation in India March*, 1992 : 935-37.

Sharma R. P. (1992), Monitoring access to food and household food security, Approaches to monitoring access to food and household food security, FAO Committee on World Food Security, 17th Session, Rome, 23-27, March, 1992.

Shrivastava M. M. P. (1983), Drought-prone area management. *Journal of Rural Development* 12,2 : 165-81, NIRD, Hyderabad.

Shubh K. Kumar (1983), A frame work for tracing policy effects on intra household food consumption. *Food and Nutrition Bulletin* 5 (4) : 2-20.

Siamwalla and Hykin S. (1983), The World Rice Market : Structure, Conduct and Performance, *Research Report* 39 : International Food Policy Research Institute, Washington, D.C.

Sinha P. R. (1966), An analysis of food expenditure in India. *Journal of Farm Econmics* 48 : 113-23.

Singh B. (1968), Role of occupational factors in household consumption. *Indian Economic Review* 3 : 85-10.

Singh R. P. (1988), Challenges of dry farming. The Hindu Survey of Indian Agriculture : 56-57.

Singh R. P. and Ramanthan Chetty C. K. (1991), Design of cropping systems to achieve nutritional goals in Dry farming. All India Coordinate Research Project for Dryland Agriculture. Hyderabad, India.

Snedocor G. W. and Cochran W. G. (1967), Statistical methods, Sixth edition. Oxford and IBH Publishing and Company p. 543-68.

Snehalatha B. (1988), Income expenditure and saving patterns of Rural Hosueholds in Ibrahimpatnam mandal of Ranga Reddy District, A.P. *Thesis submitted to the Andhra Pradesh Agricultural University*, Hyderabad.

Srivastava J. P., Gopita A. K. and Srivastava R. N. (1980), Anthopometric measurements of preschool children in rural population of Jhansi district. *Indian Paediatrics* 47:192-95.

Subramanyam S., Reddy K. S., Nageswar Rao R. and Padmanabha Rao P. (1993), District Plan Ananthapur, *Centre for Economics and Social Studies*, Hyderabad.

Sundarraj R. (1972), Food intakes of rural preschool children. *Indian Journal of Nutrition and Dietetics* 9 : 85.

Suresh Chandra Babu and Mithindi G. B. (1994), Household Food Security and Nutrition Monitoring. The Malawi Approach to development planning and policy Interventions, *Food policy*, IFPRI, Washington, D.C. 19(3).

Susan Horton (1993), Cost analysis of feeding and food subsidy programmes. *Food Policy, June 1993* : 192-99.

Swaminathan M. C., Visweswara Rao K. and Hanumantha Rao (1967), Food and nutrition in the drought areas of Andhra Pradesh. *Indian Journal of Medical Research* 55(7) : 768-78.

Swaminathan M. C., Visweswara Rao K. and Hanumantha Rao D. (1969), Food and Nutrition situation in the drought affected areas of Bihar. *Journal of Nutrition and Dietetics* 6 : 209-17.

Swaminathan M. C., Vijaya Raghavan K and Hanumanthan Rao D. (1973), Nutritional status of refuges from Bangaladesh. *Indian Journal of Med. Research* 61(2) : 278-84.

Swaminatan M. S. (1985), *Essentials of Food and Nutrition,* Volume 1:757-67.

Swaminthan M. S. (1986), Sustaining nutrion securty in Africa : lessons from Asia, Agricultural Situation in India, XLI, 5 : 279-97.

Swaminathan M. S. (1990), Presidential address given on the silver jubilee celebrations of the Directorate of Rice Research, Hyderabad held on November 14th, 1990.

Tackling Rural Poverty common wealth currents, August/September, 1992.

Teklu T., Braun J. V. and Zaki E. (1992), Drought and famine relationships in Sudan : Policy implications. *IFPRI Research Report 88,* Washington, D.C.

Thimmayamma, Parvathi Rao, Desai V. K. and Jayaprakash B. S. (1976), A study of changes in the socio-economic condition, dietary intake and nutritional status of rural families over a decade. *Ecology of Food and Nutrition* 5 : 235.

Thiammaya B. V. S., Parvati and Visweswara Rao K. (1982), Socio-economic status, Diet and Nutrient adequacies of different population groups in urban and rural Hyderabad. *The Indian Journal of Nutrition and Dietetics* 19(6) : 173-83.

Thomas J. M. (1979), On strategies and programmes for coping with large scale food shortages. *Ecology of Food and Nutrition* 8 : 209-18.

Thomas S. Walker and James G. Ryan (1990), 'Village and Household Economics in India's Semi-arid Tropics'. The Johns Hopkins University Press, Baltimore and London.

UNICEF Policy Review (1990), Strategy for improved nutrition of children and women in developing country, June 1, p.1.

Utsa P (1991), Food Availability and Famine : A longer view. *The Journal of Peasant Studies* 19,1:1-25.

Venkateswarlu J. (1992), Disaster management - A national perspective, *Kurukshetra*, December 1992 : 15-17.

Vijaya Raghavan K., Singh D. and Swaminathan M. C. (1971), Weight of well to do Indian pre-school children. *Indian Journal of Medical Research* 59 : 648.

Vijaya Raghavan K., Singh D. and Swaminathan M. C. (1974), Arm circumference and fat-fold at triceps in well nourished Indian school children. *Indian Journal of Medical Research* 62 : 994-1001.

Vijaya Raghavan K., Hanumantha Rao D., Brahmam G. N. V. and Rameshwar Sharma K. V. (1989), Assessment of Nutritional Status. NIN, ICMR, Hyderabad.

Virmani S. M. (1988), Rain forecast as a vital tool. *The Hindu Survey of Indian Agriculture* : 235.

Vyavasaya Panchangam (1994-95), Agricultural Information Centre, Andhra Pradesh Agricultural University, Hyderabad.

Watelow J. C. (1973), Note on the assessment and classification of protein energy malnutrition in children. *Lancet* 2 : 87-89.

Waterlow J. C. (1976), Classification and definition of protein-energy malnutrition. Pages 530-50 in Nutrition in preventive medicine; the major deficiency synderomes, epidemiology and approaches to control (*eds. G.H. Beaton and J.M. Bengoa*), Geneva, WHO.

Waterlow J. C., Buzina R., Kaller W., Hame J. M., Nichman M. Z. and Tanner J. M. (1977), The presentation and use of height and weight data for comparing the nutritional status of groups of children under the age of 10 years. *Bulletin of World Health Organisation* 55 : 489-98.

White Head R. G. (1979), Infact feeding practices and development of malnutrition in Rural Gambia. Food in Nutrition Bulletin 1(4) : 36-41.

Woal A. D. E. (1988), A reassessment of entitlement theory in the light of recent famines in Africa, *Development Studies working papers, International Development Centre*, Queen Elizabeth House, Oxford (1988).

Webb P., Braun J. V. and Yohannes Y. (1992), Famine in Ethiopia; policy implictaions of coping failure at Nationa and Household levels, *IFPRI, Research Report 92, International Food Policy Research Institute,* Washington, D.C.

Workshop on Nutrition Situation, artoculating National Nutrition Policy (NNP) frame work, on 18th and 19th April, 1955 by Government of India, Department of Women and Child Development, Ministry of Human Resource Development, New Delhi.

W.H.O. (1983), Measuring change in nutritional status, Geneva.

POVERTY, HOUSEHOLD FOOD SECURITY AND NUTRITION IN RURAL AREAS

Index